SAFETY DOESN'T have to be DIFFICULT!

A RECIPE FOR CREATING A STRONG AND SUSTAINABLE SAFETY MANAGEMENT SYSTEM

Michael L. Miozza CSP, CPEA, CSHM

ISBN: 061582837X
ISBN-13: 9780615828374
Library of Congress Control Number: 2013910327
Michael L Miozza, Fall River, MA

Table of Contents

FIGURES

TABLES

APPENDIX

Dedication

This book is dedicated to my family, and particularly to my *lovely* wife, Susan, who has the patience of a saint and the understanding of a valued friend. To my daughter, Angela, son, Eric, their caring spouses, and my two grandchildren, Hannah and Nathan, please know how much I love you and hope and pray that you remain safe each and every day.

This book is also dedicated to the employee who fell from a rooftop approximately thirty-two feet and landed head first onto a concrete driveway. I cannot imagine how it feels to break both legs and arms and suffer the terrific head trauma that he experienced. He was truly lucky to survive this fall. What I do know, is how horrible safety professionals feel, when this type of serious accident happens on their watch. Perhaps you are curious about how and why this person's fall protection equipment failed. Well, it didn't fail! Then you might wonder why he didn't put his equipment on. Well, unfortunately, he was *never* provided the necessary equipment. You may ask why a billion and a half dollar corporation could not afford to buy him fall protection equipment. But the company could very easily afford the equipment. Managers simply thought that they could not afford the time it took to set up and put on the fall protection equipment. The company leaders felt they would lose their competitive edge in the marketplace if they spent time on safety measures. So they elected to take chances with his safety and the safety of a large number of employees who engaged in this roof activity on a daily basis. It should *never* have happened! The company *failed* this employee. The safety management system *failed*! Unfortunately, in some companies, safety only happens by *accident*!

And lastly, this book is dedicated to the small percentage of safety professionals around the globe who may work for an employer that does *not* value safety. Please don't get too terribly discouraged. There are much easier and less stressful jobs than being a safety professional, but this is the profession you chose. Unfortunately, many companies have trouble moving beyond existing safety performance levels. When management places barriers to a safe workplace (sometimes inadvertently) – like metaphorically placing a wall of separation between themselves and safety - this "wall" can make the safety professional's job very difficult. You have a duty, an obligation, not only to the employees and organization you serve, but also to yourself, to find a way to "climb up and over the wall" and then knock the wall down. You don't need to be a "yes man" to management. If you do not agree with a safety position management takes, don't give in, fight for what you believe. Safety professionals must operate in the no-mans-land between management and the employees. Never choose sides – rather in all cases, do what is right from a safety standpoint. Leave your fingerprints on as much as you possibly can. And when you have to (and you'll know the time), move on to your next opportunity.

Acknowledgments

I offer special thanks to two exceptional individuals whom I have had the absolute and distinct pleasure of working with and mentoring over the past few years: Ms. Angela Cidade and Mr. Shaun Galligan. Shaun wrote the foreword, and Angela helped put together a PowerPoint presentation that is the foundation for this book. These two young professionals genuinely care about others' well-being and have always valued people over profits. I hope that these two talented and bright people stay in the safety field, because they will each have such a positive impact on the profession.

I also extend special mention to my client, Spindle City Insulation, Inc., and the company owners, Barbara and Michael Dubuque, who inadvertently hatched the idea for the iforSafety methodology. Barbara's call, after they had experienced a workplace injury, led me to write down the process I use for creating a safety management system. As I compiled the elements of my process, I noticed that many of the elements started with the letter *i*. Huh, I thought…*I* for safety…sounds pretty catchy to me. Only time will tell.

About the Author

Michael L. Miozza CSP, CPEA, CSHM, has directed the environmental, health, and safety systems for several major corporations. Michael has over twenty years of experience in the areas of regulatory compliance, human resource management, manufacturing, construction, business management, ISO 14001 implementation, public safety, loss prevention, and developing safety processes. His career has afforded him the opportunity to work in national and international organizations, managing multiple locations. Michael enjoys sharing his distinct perspective on leading health and safety with others.

Through a unique blend of work experiences with several major corporations, Michael has witnessed the core of high performance safety cultures. For over twenty years, Michael has successfully faced the challenges of leading injury prevention strategies with a large workforce in high-demand industries.

Michael began his safety career in 1993 working for a Fortune 100 company as a safety officer. As an insurance inspector, he has conducted hundreds of inspections ranging from general scheduled audits to serious accident investigations.

Michael is nationally recognized as a Certified Safety Professional (CSP), a Certified Professional Environmental Auditor (CPEA), and a Certified Safety and Health Manager (CSHM). He is also a professional member of the American Society of Safety Engineers, and he is a member of the National Fire Protection Association and the American Industrial Hygiene Association. He is an authorized OSHA Outreach Trainer for General Industry and Construction Safety Training for ten- and thirty-hour courses.

Michael is the founder of Health and Safety Solutions, Inc. (HSS), a safety consulting company based in Fall River, Massachusetts, and the creator of the safety management process called iforSafety. HSS is a provider of health, safety, and environmental compliance solutions. The company offers affordable solutions for all-sized organizations and business owners. HSS can help create a safe, healthy, engaged workplace, encouraging safety consciousness and promoting wellness throughout any organization. Working with management, HSS can help improve the health and safety of employees—and the bottom line. In June 2012, Health and Safety Solutions, Inc. opened the Best Practices Safety Institute in Fall River. For more information, please visit health-safetysolutions.com or call toll free (855) 785-8562.

FOREWORD

As a young safety professional, I had the opportunity to work for two very large global companies. The safety management systems at the two companies were very different from each other. One company (Company A) valued safety, had a clear vision, and supported the system from top-level management down. The other company (Company B) tried to implement safety from the middle of the organization.

The safety system at Company B was ineffective. Individuals at the bottom of the organization did not buy into the safety culture because top-level management did not support the system. Safety was a façade for Company B that only gave the illusion to federal organizations such as Occupational Safety and Health Administration (OSHA), that an effective safety system was implemented at the corporation.

Speaking with a family member, of an employee from Company B who had suffered a serious injury, was a life-changing experience. Our conversation truly affected me and it will always have a profound impact on how I view safety in the future. I already thought my heart was at its lowest point when I went to the hospital to see the injured employee. But when I saw his family, it sank even lower.

Occupational health and safety should not be viewed as simply a requirement placed upon employers by federal regulatory agencies such as OSHA. Employers should view safety as the right thing to do for their employees.

Safety should be factored in with all aspects of business—including operational procedures, cost of operations, and the bottom line (total profit)—when making executive decisions.

Having a fully implemented safety management system will help reduce the potential of OSHA citations and fines, and it will also help mitigate the potential for employee injuries. Employees will have higher morale because they will feel valued when the leadership of their company shows interest in employee safety and well-being. Employees will become engaged in the safety system because they will see the system is driven from top-level management down, and then the safety culture will begin to consume the entire workforce.

This book will describe how to create and implement a fully operational safety management system. It will not only help companies create safety systems, but it will also help companies look at their safety systems from all angles and ensure that they have captured all aspects of an effective safety system.

Shaun P. Galligan CESCO

Preface

"The time is always right to do what is right."
—Martin Luther King Jr.

I was hoping that the title, *Safety Doesn't Have to Be Difficult!* would catch your eye. The title was purposely chosen to be a little provocative and a whole lot thought provoking. "Safety doesn't have to be difficult" is not necessarily a precise statement, though. Safety can be *difficult*. And depending on the organization, it can be very difficult! I know safety can be a challenge because I have been a safety practitioner for over twenty years and I have worked with various types of organizations. Some may think that safety is very easy and think it's just simply a matter of making sure people don't get hurt on the job. It is a lot whole harder than that! It can be a struggle to achieve a safe organization that is capable of sustained safe performance in the face of significant hazards and the vast number of safety regulations. But it can and has been done.

First let me establish what safety is. In my view, safety is about local, state, and federal laws; it's about frustration and celebration; it encompasses physics, chemistry, and ergonomics, to name a few of the sciences; it involves illness and injuries; it requires money and resources; it's about attitude, accountability, and audits; it's about lockout/tagout, hazard communication, and machine guarding, to name a few of the OSHA standards; it entails risk, hazards, and corrective action; it involves culture, climate, and conflict; it's about senior management, employees, and supervisors; it's about engineering, education, and enforcement; it consists of inspections, incident investigations, and incentives; it's about first aid, fire extinguishers, and fall protection; it's about NFPA, EPA, DOT, and all other agencies and organizations that touch on safety; it requires patience, balance, and compromise; it's about citations, penalties, and violations; it involves people, property, product and partnerships; it's about weather, fire, terrorism, and other types of emergencies; it's about leadership, legalese, and leverage; it touches on ADA, FMLA, and HIPPA regulations, to name a few; it's about contractors and visitors and workplace violence and worker compensation; it enmeshes wellness programs and post-injury management systems; it usually necessitates documentation, discipline, and discharge; it's about measurement, metrics, and motivation; it embodies the legal, medical, and fire disciplines, to name a few; it's about alcohol, drugs, and substance abuse; it's about amputations, electrocutions, and suffocations; it can entail industrial hygiene and indoor air quality; it's about forklifts, ladders, and personal protective equipment; it includes policies, procedures, and guidelines; it addresses behaviors, benchmarking, and barriers; it deals with continuous improvement, consistency, and communication; it includes systems, programs, and regulation; it's about seconds and inches; and safety should never take a day off.

While this list may not incorporate all that safety is, I felt it was important to end the list with this statement: safety is about life and death. When it comes to safety, dying is not an option.

Being a safety practitioner has not always been easy for me. But what I discovered along the way is that having a system in place makes the safety function a whole lot easier. I want to emphasize, though, that safety is much more than just putting a safety management system (SMS) in place. **It is about *leadership*.** Leaders in an organization influence the activities, systems, and culture that produce the safety outcomes needed to drive safety performance. Leadership will drive the SMS in your organization. Without leadership there can be no effective and sustainable safety management system.

Jim Rohn is one of America's leading authorities on business success and a well-known business philosopher. One of my favorite Rohn quotes regarding leadership is, "Leadership is the challenge to be something more than average."[1] Leaders that drive the safety management system will see more than just average results. They will see employees totally engaged in the safety process, they will see a significant reduction in workers compensation expense and they will see an increase in productivity and profits. This book describes the best practices that create safety success for real-life organizations and provides all the ingredients needed to ensure your SMS is successful.

Reviewing the literature available, one will find that safety professionals often disagree on language and words. Safety events in the workplace may be called accidents or incidents; some discuss whether a company has a safety climate, a safety culture, or both; some debate the difference between a safety program and a safety system; others contrast a safety audit with a safety inspection. All of these are good discussions, but at the end of the day I feel we spend way too much time debating these topics. I particularly feel that these debates about semantics can be confusing to the new and young safety professional. This book

---

[1] "Excerpts from The Treasury of Quotes Success Books." ©1993, 2010 Jim Rohn International: 5.

xviii   SAFETY DOESN'T HAVE TO BE DIFFICULT!

attempts to discuss some of those differences and provide clarity in the vernacular we use in the safety profession. Some may not agree with my opinion, and that's OK, because as Kingsley Amis once said, "If you can't annoy somebody, there's little point in writing." While it is not my intent to annoy, I certainly hope the reader will appreciate and recognize the value of my point of view.

I believe most business owners and CEOs genuinely care about the safety and well-being of their employees. However, there will always be businesses that place profits ahead of employee safety. I know this firsthand

> Sometimes **nothing positive happens** until something negative happens to change an organization's view of safety.

because I worked in such an organization for a number of years. The experience of working for both caring companies and a company that placed little value on safety provides me invaluable perspective.

We know that all organizations face risks associated with their activities. Today's organizations operate in a complex and challenging environment that must be carefully managed and monitored to assure safety at all levels. According to the National Safety Council publication, *Injury Facts*, 2013 edition, in 2011, a worker fatality occurred every 134 minutes in our country. On average, 12 working people a day died—every day—for 365 days. I find that statistic totally unacceptable, because I believe there is no job worth dying for! If you have been concerned about safety in your organization, if you have tossed and turned some nights, then now is the time to focus on your safety management system.

Believe it or not, there are organizations where safety professionals feel senior management does not value safety. I ask, where's the shame in working safe? In a June 2010 poll conducted by the

National Safety Council, more than 14 percent of respondents said senior management does not value safety. Obviously these organizations do not have a safety management system in place. It is difficult for health and safety professionals to generate enthusiasm for safety or to revamp their safety system when senior management assumes little responsibility for the protection of workers' health and safety.

While sad but true, sometimes nothing positive happens until something negative happens to change an organization's view of safety. A huge OSHA fine or a fatality can encourage an organization to improve its safety performance. Companies need to recognize that worker safety is not a cost of doing business but an investment. When done properly, safety pays big dividends. Worker safety must not and should *never* be a matter of luck.

To those of us who have been following OSHA news over the past few years, it is clear that things have changed at the agency. By now we all have some idea of what we can expect from the new OSHA. Since 2008, we have seen OSHA move from partnership with business to toughening its enforcement philosophy. The record $87.4 million citation issued against BP North America Texas City refinery in 2009 demonstrates this change in philosophy. OSHA has become energized, revitalized, and focused on a host of new enforcement initiatives. What is the outlook for 2013 and beyond? It appears OSHA's regulatory priority remains its Injury and Illness Prevention Program (I2P2). This rule would require employers to find and fix hazards in their own workplaces that are not addressed by any existing OSHA standard. During a plenary session at the American Society of Safety Engineers Safety 2013 conference in Las Vegas, OSHA Administrator Dr. David Michaels discussed his second term leading the agency and his hopes for the proposed I2P2 program. Even though he stated it is still the agency's top priority, he was not providing a timeline. When pressed for I2P2's possible progress, Michael's' was unable to provide concrete dates, and said he was "hesitant to predict anything."[2] If OSHA gets I2P2 passed it will be a game changer. This book will be a valuable tool to assist you in implementing I2P2.

The next few years will present a challenge for employers as the economy remains uncertain and OSHA continues to initiate new policy changes. Safety can sometimes be a battle, and to win a battle you must have a strategy. Now is the time to take a close look at your organization's safety culture to see if there are areas in which you can improve. In short, it is a good time to put your safety system under the magnifying glass and view it with a critical eye.

The frustrating part about safety is that it always seems to get measured by the negatives—accidents, near misses, workers' compensation payouts, OSHA fines, and, worst of all, fatalities.

> Just because someone **does not get hurt on the job** does not mean that the workplace is safe.

Wouldn't it be better if safety could be measured by positive outcomes that go well beyond the absence of an accident or incident? What if there really was a way to change the measuring stick, so that employers could be more effective in preventing injuries *before* they happen? That is what an effective safety management system can do for you and your organization.

The safety of employees should be a primary concern in the day-to-day operations for business owners and managers. Successful companies create a protected and hazard-free work environment for employees and customers. The more comfortable and confident a company's employees are, the more productive those employees will be, which increases the

---

[2] Walter, Laura. "OSHA Administrator Michaels calls I2P2 Highest Priority." *EHS Today*, June 26, 2013. http://ehstoday.com/osha/safety-2013.

output and profitability of the business. Creating this safe work environment requires implementing a safety management system.

> No one ever plans to go to work to get hurt or die. And yet it happens! It has been said that life is full of second chances, but you may have **only** one chance - with your life -when it comes to safety. Safety should **never** be a matter of *chance.*

The development of a strong and sustainable safety system can be difficult for business owners and human resource professionals who do not understand or are unaware of state and federal workplace regulations. Furthermore, mere adherence to those regulations does not necessarily represent an optimally safe, hazard-free, and comfortable working environment for employees.

The recent downsizing of many companies due to the economic changes has often placed the management of occupational health and safety programs on human resource professionals or business owners, who lack the benefit of experience or education in this field.

As the CEO, human resource person responsible for safety, or business owner, you have the responsibility of managing your company's safety programs. Congratulations! But what do you do and where do you start? Safety is a full-time job considering the numerous safety-related areas you need to be aware of: safety procedures, worker training, OSHA standards, reasonable accommodations, workers' compensation, accident investigations, GHS, recordkeeping, return-to-work issues, safety committees, various written forms...and the list goes on and on.

In 2010, a survey by the University of Chicago's National Opinion Research Center (NORC) of 1,461 workers found that 85 percent of workers ranked "workplace safety regulations" as *the* **number one labor standard issue,** above family and maternity leave, minimum wage, paid sick days, overtime pay, and the right to join a union. Despite the finding, the authors noted that "media coverage of workplace safety issues has been sporadic and evaluations of public attention to the issue even rarer."

SOURCE: Public Attitudes Towards and Experiences with Workplace Safety, was prepared by Dr. Tom W. Smith at the National Opinion Research Center at the University of Chicago for the Public Welfare Foundation. August, 2010.

Do you want to acquire insight on how to create a strong and sustainable safety management system? This book was written to help those individuals charged with the responsibility for improving or initiating a new safety management system. Whether you are a safety department of one, a human resource manager that has been given safety responsibilities, or a business owner who has little experience with managing safety systems, this book will provide the necessary ingredients you will need to create and sustain an effective SMS. While it may seem daunting, please understand that it does not need to be difficult. There is an old saying I have used frequently throughout my career: "Proper planning prevents poor performance."

Plan your safety management system to prevent poor performance. You will be creating a safety system that will reduce the number of injuries in your organization and most certainly improve employee morale. Read the book from cover to cover. But remember—*action,* not words in a book, prevents injuries. It's time to turn insight into action.

Don't allow your organization to become part of the OSHA statistics in a negative way. Spice up your SMS. A quote attributed to Albert Einstein is, "insanity: doing the same thing over and over again and expecting different results." Instead, master the twelve ingredients outlined in this book. These ingredients will significantly contribute to building a strong and sustainable SMS for your organization. Learn the strategies that will enable you to establish an ongoing, proactive safety management system.

This book is an introduction to managing safety. Job safety and health is the law of the land. Know that OSHA standards are the absolute minimum safety standards an organization must comply with. These rules create a baseline that all employers are required to meet.[3] Every employer that comes under OSHA jurisdiction must post in the workplace the free Job Safety and Health poster available from OSHA (see Appendix E). This poster outlines both employers' and employees' safety responsibilities under the law and serves as the foundation for creating a safety management system. Additionally, Appendix J outlines OSHA's Safety and Health Management Guidelines, which the agency believes can reduce the extent and severity of work-related injuries and illnesses and their related costs. Let me make one comment about OSHA here. If you think OSHA means, "Our Savior Has Arrived," you will be disappointed. OSHA is grossly understaffed and underbudgeted. In the United States, there are approximately 2,000 federal and state OSHA inspectors to cover more than seven million workplaces. They are responsible for the health and safety of over 130 million workers, which translates to about one compliance and health officer for every 60,000 workers. [4] According

[3] Stricoff, Scott R. and Donald R. Goover. "The Manager's Guide to Workplace Safety." California: BST, 2012.
[4] Moran, Mark. "The OSHA Answer Book, 10th Edition." Copyright ©2011 Moran Associates, Inc.

to a report by AFL–CIO, it would take OSHA 129 years to inspect all workplaces under its jurisdiction.[5] Furthermore, the agency recently has been too focused on punishment and not enough on prevention. That said, going to work day in and day out may still be dangerous to your health and safety given the number of injuries, illnesses, and deaths that still occur in our country year after year. Given this fact, I unequivocally believe that it is the duty of employers—*not* OSHA—to protect workers' health and safety.

To help the reader delve deeper into safety management systems and the value systems offer, I have included in Appendix A, a partial list of some books that are part of my professional library. These authors have been instrumental in framing my beliefs about the value of a strong and sustainable SMS in protecting employees' well-being and teaching organizations how to improve safety performance.

If you are new to safety, this book will help you understand OSHA standards and what OSHA does, learn what OSHA records you need to maintain, comprehend why it is important to identify safety hazards in your workplace, appreciate why you need to conduct workplace job hazard analysis, see the value in performing regular workplace inspections and auditing your SMS, recognize why conducting thorough incident investigations is so very important, know what workers' compensation is and how it affects your safety management system, be a safety leader and achieve buy-in from all levels of your organization, and learn what you can do right now to grow a safety culture in your workplace.

My goal is to provide the reader reality-based and practical advice about safety management systems. There is no one-size-fits-all

---

[5] "Death on the Job: the Toll of Neglect, 20th Edition." April, 2011. AFL-CIO. http://www.aflcio.org/content/download/6485/69821/dotj_2011.pdf.

solution for changing a safety culture, but this book will offer you the safety insights you need, to create a solid foundation for a strong and sustainable safety management system. It will tell you how to stay on top of the safety laws, rules, and regulations that apply to your organization. It will provide many, many tips for systematizing your safety program to increase efficiency, effectiveness, and sustainability. This book provides strategies for generating management commitment to, and employee support for, a strong workplace safety system. It will help you assess the impact injuries and illnesses have on the company's profitability, which will allow you to justify additional safety resources, staff, or departmental involvement. It will tell you why it's crucial to integrate safety into day-to-day operations and how to go about this. It provides practical, simple methods to assess and audit your SMS on an ongoing basis and correct any problems you find. Throughout this book, I used valuable insight from my own personal experiences in the various industries where I have worked to demonstrate the concepts presented. I did not create anything new. Instead, I packaged what was already in the literature, along with over twenty years of my own personal experiences and my formal education, into a safety management system that I call iforSafety. And, finally, this book will inform you what to do when you encounter a challenge that goes beyond your level of expertise, by directing you to resources for guidance and answers.

A recipe is a set of instructions for cooking or preparing a particular food.[6] A recipe tells you what ingredients you need to use and in what amounts. Much like a recipe, when creating a safety management system, you need a set of instructions, and you need to know what ingredients to use and in what amounts, so you can properly prepare your safety system. Allow me to share my recipe with you.

---

[6] "Bing Dictionary." 2013 Microsoft Corporation.

Chapter 1

What is the Current Regulatory Climate?

Worker safety must not and should never be a matter of "luck"!
—MICHAEL L. MIOZZA

There were 4,609 work-related deaths in 2011[7] and millions more suffered nonfatal injuries at work.[8] This works out to an average of twelve deaths per day. Employers pay an estimated $1 billion per week for direct workers' compensation costs.[9] The health and safety of workers in the workplace may be a primary concern for business owners, but many do not have the personnel or skills necessary to provide adequate safety.

[7] US Bureau of Labor Statistics. "Census of Fatal Occupational Injuries Summary 2011 USDL-12-1888." (September 20, 2012).
[8] US Bureau of Labor Statistics. "Workplace Injury and Illness Summary 2011 USDL-12-2121." (October 25, 2012).
[9] "2012 Liberty Mutual Workplace Safety Index" [PDF* - 848 KB, 2 pages]. Liberty Mutual Insurance Company. (2012).

Because advances are being made in occupational health and safety on industry, state, and federal levels, meeting base regulations is simply not enough in today's rapidly developing markets. Businesses have to create and maintain sustainable safety systems—not only to meet regulatory standards—but also to instill confidence in employees and promote better productivity and output.

> **OSHA's General Duty Clause** states that, "each employer shall furnish to each of his employees employment and a place of employment which are free from recognized hazards that are causing or are likely to cause death or serious physical harm to his employees."

This book is in no way intended to be political in nature; however it does warrant mentioning there was an obvious change in the regulatory climate in President Obama's first term. This was evident when shortly after Hilda Solis was confirmed as the new Secretary of Labor, she pledged to "put enforcement back into the Department of Labor."

The confirmation of Dr. David Michaels as Assistant Secretary of Labor for OSHA in December 2009 was another significant health and safety development. If one looks back at Michaels's 2007 congressional testimony, he claimed at the time that, "OSHA does not work for people" and that "it is broken." As the nation's point man for safety, we saw a newfound aggressiveness from OSHA, backed by the Secretary of Labor. Michaels has pushed for an OSHA standard requiring worksites to have a safety and health program currently known as I2P2. Under his leadership, it has been a new day for safety, as Dr. Michaels attempts to initiate new safety rules and the agency flexes its enforcement muscles by issuing fines to companies nationwide for smaller violations.[10]

---

[10] Tech Environmental e-Newsletter September 2010. "OSHA Fines Double Under New Leadership." http://www.techenv.com/E-News/Enews0910.htm.

Solis and Michaels were the new sheriffs at OSHA who were ready to make the agency more assertive. They had an aggressive agenda for rulemaking, were placing more emphasis on enforcement, and were significantly increasing penalties. This would include more OSHA inspections conducted in the coming years. There was absolutely no question OSHA had changed radically and had moved in a different direction. Despite OSHA's renewed focus on enforcement and setting standards, the agency was still committed to offering compliance assistance to employers.

In December 2009, OSHA was provided with one of the largest budget increases it had received in recent years. The $558.6

> On October 20, 2009, OSHA issued **a record $87.4 million dollar fine** to BP for alleged failure to correct hazards at its Texas City refinery.

million allocated to OSHA was about 8 percent more than the agency received in its FY2009 budget. This increased funding went toward hiring more than one hundred additional compliance inspectors. Additionally, OSHA intensified its enforcement efforts by making increased use of corporate-wide settlement agreements and rolling out a program for egregious violators, known as the Severe Violator Enforcement Program.[11] It was apparent that OSHA had become more aggressive as it pushed for more and stronger enforcement.

> **OSHA regulations** are in place for one main reason: to prevent employees from being injured. Remember, though, that OSHA regulations are the absolute minimum requirements that an organization must follow.

To respond to the ailing economy, Congress passed the American Recovery and Reinvestment Act of 2009. This was an economic stimulus package, particularly for construction projects. Due to this influx of cash, the country

[11] Sean, Ryan. "OSHA vows strong stimulus presence." *The Daily Reporter* (May 14, 2009). http://dailyreporter.com/blog/2009/05/14/osha-vows-strong-stimulus-presence/.

saw more construction projects than usual, which prompted the need for increased health and safety supervision. While contractors had mixed reactions, most felt that more management would be beneficial for safer operations.[12] An example of OSHA's renewed emphasis on enforcement was the record $87.4 million citation issued against BP North America Texas City refinery in 2009. The BP fine and other record-breaking OSHA fines in the news were eye-popping.[13]

Since the start of the Great Recession in December 2007, the world has seen major political changes and experienced economic challenges. It has been a demanding business environment. In today's uncertain economy, lean is key. Getting management buy-in for safety spending has always been difficult—and in a bad economy it is even tougher. Businesses are asking employees to do more with less—increasing their responsibilities, asking them to take on unfamiliar jobs, and asking them to work longer hours—all of which can increase the risk of accidents. And yet safety is often one of the first areas to be cut. But just because the economy stinks does not mean management should give up on creating or improving an SMS, because managing risks has its rewards. In fact, it would be a smart move to invest in safety right now given OSHA's new funding levels and new initiatives. Organizations can manage safety successfully with reduced resources.

Toward the end of Obama's first term, the political climate radically changed. OSHA was under attack and being accused by elected officials of killing jobs in our country. How unfair! In my humble opinion, based on my firsthand experience working for several Fortune 500 companies and with OSHA, lawmakers need to strengthen the

---

[12] "OSHA Proposes to Fine BP $87.4 Million for Continuing Violations at Texas Refinery." (39 OSHR 935, November 5, 2009).

[13] *Job Safety and Health.* The Bureau of National Affairs, Inc., no. 420 (April 9, 2013).

agency's enforcement powers. With so few compliance and health officers, with so many businesses under their jurisdiction, and with penalties for non-compliance so small, it is no wonder that organizations have little fear of OSHA.

Others charged that OSHA regulations cost businesses money. This assault on OSHA seemed to take the wind out of OSHA and Obama's sails. In January 2013 Solis tendered her resignation as Labor Secretary. In March 2013 President Obama nominated Assistant Attorney General Thomas E. Perez to replace Solis. Michaels will stay at his post.

The 2013 OSHA budget was $565.5 million, which represented only a $680,470 increase over OSHA's 2012 budget. In early 2013, due to the budget sequestration called for in the Budget Control Act, OSHA's budget was deeply cut by $46 million. The budget sequestration means OSHA's enforcement activity will be inhibited, as well as its regulatory activity.

However, even given the current unstable economy, OSHA is still trying to shape its proposed rule—I2P2—that would require employers to develop a formal safety program to reduce workplace injuries and illnesses through a systematic process that proactively addresses workplace safety and health hazards. Many hope that OSHA will try to move forward

President Richard Nixon signed the **Occupational Safety and Health Act into law** on December 29, 1970, creating OSHA, which set out to *"assure safe and healthful working conditions for working men and women by setting and enforcing standards and providing training, outreach, education and assistance."*

with I2P2 during Obama's second term. Should I2P2 pass, OSHA will change the way companies conduct business for safety and health.

OSHA faces a number of challenges beyond 2013. The investigation into the West Fertilizer Plant explosion in West, Texas, on April 17, 2013 that killed fourteen people and injured at least two hundred will certainly bring into question regulatory oversight and whether the facility had systems in place to prevent or minimize this type of tragedy. The explosion was so massive that it registered as a 2.1 magnitude earthquake. A team from the U.S. Chemical Safety Board was sent to investigate.[14] Even in the year 2013 we are still experiencing serious and deadly industrial accidents.

I strongly believe that employers and business owners should assess their workplaces today to make certain that their safety systems, at the very minimum, meet the OSHA standards. Workplaces with high injury and illness rates are still in OSHA sights. Whether your organization is big or small, OSHA demands a lot of you. And, if you fall short, you can face costly penalties and fines, or, even more tragically, serious employee injuries or deaths. Don't roll the dice with your employee's safety, because worker safety must not and should never be a matter of luck.

---

[14] Irwin, Alex. *Safety Compliance Alert Resource Center.* (April 2013).

Chapter 2

What is a Safety Culture?

**One person caring about another represents
life's greatest value.**
—JIM ROHN

There is no one single definition of a "safety culture." Like the air we breathe, one cannot see it. Every organization has a safety culture, even if it is not good. Cultures are most commonly defined as common practices, shared attitudes, and perceptions that influence behavioral choices at work and away. Experience has taught me that several things influence a culture, such as location, leadership, supervisory styles, peer pressure, workplace conditions, and logistics, to name a few.

> **Safety is a whole lot more** than dealing with OSHA regulations and a whole lot more than good intentions.
>
> **Safety is the confidence** employees have in their organizational leaders, that these leaders are truly committed to ensuring serious incidents are not likely to happen in their work environment.

A safety culture is often described as "how we do things when no one is looking." For example, when a worker faithfully wears his or her hard hat or safety glasses, or a construction worker always places the ladder three feet past the roof line when the supervisor is not around, then the safety culture is generally said to be sound. Safety cultures develop and change over rather long periods of time. Strong managers and/or safety professionals leave their mark on an organization's culture. Conversely, though, the absence of such persons can also influence the culture.

OSHA defines a Total Safety Culture (TSC) as a culture where everyone feels responsible for safety and pursues it on a daily basis - employees go beyond the call of duty to identify unsafe conditions and behaviors, and they intervene to correct them. OSHA believes that all elements of a safety and health system are interrelated. A flaw in one area will likely impact all other areas, and therefore the system as a whole. [15]

It has been my experience that there are two indispensable ingredients of a sound safety culture. They are management commitment and employee engagement. If you don't have both, you cannot—will not—have a sound safety culture.

You should take a close look at your organization's safety culture, or lack thereof. Here are some attributes of a sound safety culture:

- Management is visible and follows the safety rules.
- Management wisely invests in safety.

---

[15] *"What is this thing called culture?"*   eTools Home: Safety & Health Management Systems. http://www.osha.gov/SLTC/etools/safetyhealth/mod2_culture.html. Retrieved July 18, 2013.

- Safety is on equal footing with other company core values.
- Safety terms are part of the language of the organization.
- Workplace safety is part of everyone's job description.
- Safe and unsafe behaviors are specified and enforced.
- People are recognized in a visible way for promoting safety.
- Safety is evident in the interaction among employees.
- New employees are trained on safety and its impact.
- Employees observe and report hazards and corrective action is taken.
- Employees "dress for success" by using appropriate personal protective equipment (PPE).
- Employees buy in to the idea that safety is part of their job.
- Workplace incidents are investigated in a timely manner.
- All employees know the consequences of ignoring safety practices.

Assessing an organization's safety culture often provides valuable, actionable insight for those individuals who are serious about achieving and sustaining safety excellence. Through an assessment process or gap analysis, a safety culture can be measured. Once it has been measured, the safety culture can be better managed, transformed, and sustained. After review-

> ## PEARLS OF WISDOM
>
> ✔ All organizations have a safety culture.
>
> ✔ Without management commitment and employee engagement you cannot create a positive safety culture.
>
> ✔ Assessing your safety culture by conducting safety perception surveys will tell you your specific strengths and weaknesses.
>
> ✔ It takes time to develop or change a safety culture.

ing the assessment's significant findings, identify and prioritize the critical few findings that have the potential for the greatest transformational impact on improving the organization or site's safety culture.

Should safety be the most important company value? BS, I say. I don't believe it should ever be the number one priority; it should be *one of the company's priorities*, and on equal footing with other core company values. We've all seen company core safety values prominently posted on signs in facilities and lunchrooms that promote "Safety is priority number one." But how many companies actually walk the talk and include safety among their core values? At your workplace, is safety a true way of life? Or is it just something that's paid lip service at best? As a safety manager or person responsible for safety, you may have heard someone at your company say something like the following, usually after an incident or near miss, "We need to improve our safety culture." The problem is that a safety culture isn't something you can just pick up at a safety store like a new batch of gloves or safety glasses. It's something that needs to run deeply through your organization at all levels—something that goes beyond mere lip service and inspirational "safety first" posters. You can transform your culture by implementing a practical safety management system. But know that employing an SMS does not necessarily mean that you now automatically have a safety culture. A safety culture is about values, belief systems, feelings, and perceptions. And it can take a considerable amount of time to cultivate the safety culture you desire.

Developing an effective safety culture employs a simple philosophy, namely, that working safely is a cultural issue. An effective safety culture will eventually lead to the desired goal of zero incidents in the workplace, and this book will provide an understanding of what is needed to help reach this goal. I provide reference material for all phases of building an SMS and ultimately developing a safety management system that fits the organization's culture. Know that a safety culture takes time to take root. Safety should not be separate from other standard operating procedures, but quite often it is. Integrating safety with other core company values will make the process easier.

A review of the literature suggests that there is a difference among safety professionals between the terms *safety culture* and *safety climate*. In a doctoral thesis by Steven Yule, entitled *Safety Culture and Safety Climate: A Review of the Literature*, the author's research clearly indicates that safety climate is distinct from safety culture. Mr. Yule concludes that, "Culture seems far more important in determining who we are, and why we behave in certain ways, whereas climate can be seen as more of a reflection of what we are and what we do."[16]

I think that a good safety culture is very much like a good meal. It's the right combination of many ingredients that will get you a great dish. You may get the culture you want by sheer luck (I've been employed at some of these organizations), or it may be the process of strenuous trial and error and a whole lot of experience. Like a good meal, a good safety culture is in the combination of elements and interaction. There will be some elements in one particular organization that should be stressed more than others. This differs for each organization. If I had to pick one key element to be the foundation of a good quality safety culture, I would say great leaders are very important, much like a chef is for a gourmet meal.

---

[16] S. Yule. "Senior Management Influence on Safety Performance in the UK and US Energy Sectors." PhD diss., University of Aberdeen. Scotland (2003).

Chapter 3

What are the Development Phases of a Safety Culture?

If you do not change direction, you may end up where you are heading.
—LAO TZU

An organization is a complex institution made up of people with diverse educations, skills, and experience who perform various tasks to ensure the success of the operation.[17] The challenge for the organization is to ensure people perform these tasks safely. Safety is a primary factor in managing cost and employee turnover, and it ensures business continuity. Keeping a workplace free from physical or psychological hazards can be difficult and time-consuming, especially for small business owners who may not be able to identify where and how to start. Further, ensuring a safe work environment is a business expense that does not directly contribute to the bottom line. Thus, business owners may at times be tempted to treat safety as an expense that can be trimmed.

---

[17] Swartz, George, ed. "Safety Culture and Effective Management." Chicago, Illinois: National Safety Council (NSC), 2000. 103.

However, the accidental disregard of federal or state workplace regulations can be costly, and at times disastrous, for business owners who are uncertain about or ignorant of such requirements.

As a human resource professional, a business owner, or the person responsible for safety—have you ever asked yourself—how do we build a safety culture that is compliant, lasting, and intrinsic in our operations day in and day out? There is no one-size-fits-all solution for improving a safety culture. However, by following a simple and systematic approach, companies can improve their loss experience. Implementing a safety management system is a simple and systemic way of managing your organization's health and safety affairs to improve safety performance, raise the awareness of the value of safety and improve the overall safety culture.

> On July 2, 1982, OSHA created the **Voluntary Protection Program** (VPP) to encourage outstanding site safety and health programs. VPP now exists in more than 1,400 United States work sites.

Whether it is ANSI Z10 -2012, ISO 18001, OSHA's Voluntary Protection Program (VPP), or any number of other safety systems out there, each system will provide an organization with detailed instructions and tools necessary for implementing a successful system. The success of the system implementation will help an organization comply with OSHA requirements, and it will improve performance and positively impact the bottom line. A review of the literature suggests, that successfully implementing any of these safety management systems, will have a positive impact on your company's health and safety culture.

PEARLS OF WISDOM

✓ There is no one-size-fits-all solution for improving a safety culture.

✓ Develop your safety management system based on your organization's culture.

✓ In order to understand your present safety state, conduct an assessment or gap analysis.

One of the most important safety performance improvement steps that you and your leadership team can take is to assess your safety management system by conducting a "gap analysis" of your present safety system. In chapter 20, I discuss how you can determine your current safety condition by taking a free Internet-based assessment.

While some safety practitioners say an organization's safety culture is difficult to characterize, based on my review of the literature and my own personal experience, I have found there are five distinct developmental phases that can help define a safety culture. Over time, an organization can move through all five phases.

The five developmental phases are:

1. **Indistinct:** Safety is almost nonexistent and is indistinguishable as a core function in the organization.

2. **Initiation:** Safety is based primarily on rules and regulations and is in its infancy stage.

3. **Illumination:** Safety is considered an organizational objective and there is knowledge about the benefits of safety.

4. **Insight:** Safety can always be improved and there is a solid understanding of the safety function.

5. **Inspirational:** Safety is exceptional and the system is moving in the right direction.

For a more in-depth look at the five developmental phases of a safety culture, review the table labeled "Safety Management System iChart," located at the end of this chapter.

A really fine book about safety culture and the factors the authors believe lead to safety excellence, is from global safety leader, Behavioral Science Technology, called *The Zero Index: A Path to Sustainable Safety Excellence*. In a Zero Index organization, safety performance is no longer treated as something *other*; the goals, activities, planning, and results are a natural part of the organization's overall performance, and are integrated with day-to-day business functions and decisions. Safety is *not* thought to be in opposition to business goals.[18]

THE FIVE PHASES OF A SAFETY CULTURE

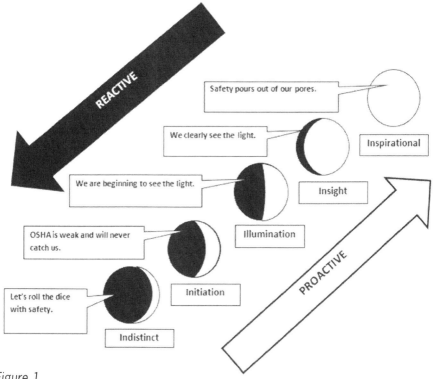

Figure 1

<hr />

[18] Colin, Duncan, General Editor and Rebecca Nigel, ed. "The Zero Index: A Path to Sustainable Safety Excellence." Ojai, California: Behavioral Science Technology (BST), 2012.

PHASE 1: INDISTINCT

At this stage an organization sees safety as an add-on. Safety is not integrated with other core business functions. Safety is an albatross around the organization's neck.

Some characteristics of an organization in Phase 1 are:

- Safety is *not* a core company value.
- Little money is spent on safety.
- Likely there is no written safety policy.
- Management tends to roll the dice with safety and they often blame employees for workplace incidents.
- Workers' compensation expense is viewed as a cost of doing business.

PHASE 2: INITIATION

At this stage there is some awareness. Management is starting to see the light.

Some characteristics of an organization in Phase 2 are:

- Senior management realizes that people must be held accountable or there is no safety.
- Senior management recognizes the need to provide safety training.
- Senior management begins to grasp that they must move past blaming employees for workplace accidents.
- Management may feel that OSHA enforcement is weak.

PHASE 3: ILLUMINATION

At this stage there is enlightenment. Supervisors understand they are responsible and accountable for safety.

Some characteristics of an organization in Phase 3 are:

- The organization starts conducting regular safety inspections.
- Safety metrics are developed for the organization.
- Safety is now part of new hire orientation.
- A safety committee is formed and meets regularly.

PHASE 4: INSIGHT

At this stage there is understanding. Senior managers are concerned about safety and are asking what they can do to improve the system.

Some characteristics of an organization in Phase 4 are:

- Supervisors now take the time to orient new hires about safety.
- Safety is discussed at senior management meetings.
- Near-miss incidents are now investigated.
- All employees are held accountable for safety.

PHASE 5: INSPIRATIONAL

At this stage both management and employees are highly motivated to have a safe workplace. Safety is seamlessly integrated with other core company values such as production, quality, and finance. The organization understands that the business benefits directly, through reduced costs, and indirectly, through improved morale and increased productivity.

Some characteristics of an organization in Phase 5 are:

- Management "walks the talk" and has a strong conviction that workplace incidents and injuries are unacceptable in their operations.
- Safety is appropriately funded.
- Management wants to lead the industry in safety.

- Safety is everyone's responsibility. Accountability at all levels of the organization.
- The company lives and breathes safety.

THE 5 DEVELOPMENTAL PHASES OF A SAFETY CULTURE				
Phase 1	Phase 2	Phase 3	Phase 4	Phase 5
Indistinct	Initiation	Illumination	Insight	Inspirational
Safety is almost nonexistent and is indistinguishable as a core function in the organization.	Safety is based primarily on rules and regulations and is in its infancy stage.	Safety is considered an organizational objective and there is knowledge about the benefits of safety.	Safety can always be improved and there is a solid understanding of the safety function.	Safety is exceptional and the system is moving in the right direction.
Safety Acuity: 20/180	Safety Acuity: 20/80	Safety Acuity: 20/20	Safety Acuity: 20/10	Safety Acuity: 20/2
Nearly blind	Corrective lenses needed	Average eyesight	Better than average	Hawk eye

Table 1

What is the condition of your safety culture? Don't be blind to what can be; *see* what can be. It is important to understand or *see* where your organization currently is in the development of a safety culture. A review of the iChart will help clarify where your safety system is currently performing. The iChart can assist you in determining your current condition and can help you start thinking about how you would like your safety system to perform in the future.

Safety Management System iChart
Developmental Phases

Ingredient	Phase 1 Indistinct	Phase 2 Initiation	Phase 3 Illumination	Phase 4 Insight	Phase 5 Inspirational
	Safety is almost nonexistent and is indistinguishable as a core function in the organization.	*Safety is based primarily on rules and regulations and is in its infancy stage.*	*Safety is considered an organizational objective and there is knowledge about the benefits of safety.*	*Safety can always be improved and there is a solid understanding of the safety function.*	*Safety is exceptional and the system is moving in the right direction.*
	Safety Acuity: 20/180 Nearly blind	**Safety Acuity: 20/80** Corrective lenses needed	**Safety Acuity: 20/20** Average eyesight	**Safety Acuity: 20/10** Better than average	**Safety Acuity: 20/2** Hawk eye
1. Invent	Workers compensation expense is considered a cost of doing business. Safety is given lip service. There is no written safety manual or policy. Senior management pays very little attention to safety.	Senior management starts to see the light. The organization creates a safety policy statement. Management takes action after an incident occurs.	Total buy-in by senior management. The organization puts their vision for safety in motion. There are clearly defined safe work policies and procedures.	Senior management asks how the safety management system can be improved. There is a real commitment to safety. Management is starting to understand the safety system.	Profound knowledge. Management looks at safety through a "different lens". Management "walks" the "talk". Very visible and leads by example. Wants to lead their industry in safety.
2. Invest	Show me the money! The organization spends little on safety. If we cannot afford safety maybe we should not be in business.	The organization starts providing resources to achieve safety standards.	Broken, defective, or improperly maintained equipment that could cause injury is promptly repaired or replaced.	Staffing is at appropriate levels. The organization realizes safety is good business.	Safety is appropriately funded. Employees are given time to do the job safely.
3. Integrate	Safety is not a core company value. Safety resides in a silo.	The organization starts to realize that safety must be integrated with production, quality and other core organizational values.	Senior management is committed to turning safety into a core company value. Line supervisors understand they are responsible and accountable for safety.	Senior management knows safety must move beyond a top priority because priorities may shift over time. Safety moves from a priority in the organization to a core company value.	Safety is seamlessly integrated with production, quality and other core company values and is on equal footing with those values.

Safety Management System iChart
Developmental Phases

Ingredient	Phase 1 Indistinct	Phase 2 Initiation	Phase 3 Illumination	Phase 4 Insight	Phase 5 Inspirational
	Safety is almost nonexistent and is indistinguishable as a core function in the organization.	Safety is based primarily on rules and regulations and is in its infancy stage.	Safety is considered an organizational objective and there is knowledge about the benefits of safety.	Safety can always be improved and there is a solid understanding of the safety function.	Safety is exceptional and the system is moving in the right direction.
	Safety Acuity: 20/180 Nearly blind	Safety Acuity: 20/80 Corrective lenses needed	Safety Acuity: 20/20 Average eyesight	Safety Acuity: 20/10 Better than average	Safety Acuity: 20/2 Hawk eye
4. Introduce	Safety is not part of the new hire orientation agenda.	There is discussion that safety should be considered when a new person is on-boarded.	Safety is now part of new hire orientation.	Supervisors take the necessary time to orient new hires about safety.	A co-worker is allowed to spend time with the new employee.
5. Involve	No established safety committee that meets regularly.	The organizations safety message is starting to be expressed as they begin providing resources for safety.	There are regular scheduled safety committee meetings. Meeting minutes are distributed to all employees.	Senior management allows employees to be totally engaged in the safety process.	Employees "see" safety as interesting, energizing and practical. Managers and employees work together on teams to constantly fix the safety system.
6. Inform	Not only does senior management not "walk" safety, they don't even "talk" about it!	Senior management discusses ways to keep employees informed about relevant safety matters.	Management provides clear communication at every level of the organization.	Safety is discussed at senior management meetings. Safety terms are part of the organizations language.	Communication is a two-way street and employees feel very comfortable talking about safety.
7. Instruct	Safety training is nearly non-existent. Management believes that all it takes for workers to be safe is a little common sense.	Senior management recognizes that knowledge is the foundation of a sound and sustainable safety system.	The organization conducts meaningful ongoing safety training.	A stronger safety culture has been built through safety training.	The organization spends significant money on training and realizes that there is a return on their investment.

Safety Management System iChart
Developmental Phases

Ingredient	Phase 1 Indistinct	Phase 2 Initiation	Phase 3 Illumination	Phase 4 Insight	Phase 5 Inspirational
	Safety is almost nonexistent and is indistinguishable as a core function in the organization.	*Safety is based primarily on rules and regulations and is in its infancy stage.*	*Safety is considered an organizational objective and there is knowledge about the benefits of safety.*	*Safety can always be improved and there is a solid understanding of the safety function.*	*Safety is exceptional and the system is moving in the right direction.*
	Safety Acuity: 20/180 Nearly blind	**Safety Acuity: 20/80 Corrective lenses needed**	**Safety Acuity: 20/20 Average eyesight**	**Safety Acuity: 20/10 Better than average**	**Safety Acuity: 20/2 Hawk eye**
8. Inspect	Safety inspections and audits are *not regularly* conducted. The organization does not have its eye on safety.	Senior management grasps the concept that workplace hazard recognition is an important ingredient of a safety management system.	The organization conducts regular safety inspections.	Regular documented safety inspections and audits occur and feedback is provided to the department manager or supervisor.	There is a commitment from management to look at the safety inspection data and provide necessary resources to quickly act on the findings. Corrective and preventive actions are initiated in a timely manner.
9. Investigate	Incidents are not sufficiently investigated.	Senior management understands that they must move past blaming employees for workplace incidents.	Incidents are thoroughly investigated for root cause.	Near misses are a wakeup call for the organization.	Every incident and near miss is thoroughly investigated.
10. Intervene	There is little progressive discipline for safety infractions. When an employee is hurt on the job there is no post injury management system in place to help the injured worker.	Senior management realizes there must be accountability for safety or there is no safety.	To reinforce safe behavior progressive discipline is issued for safety infractions.	Accountability for safety performance is established for every level of the organization. Line supervision is now accountable for safety, not just the safety manager.	Progressive discipline is consistently used to reinforce that senior management is serious about safety. There is an effective post management injury system in place.

Safety Management System iChart
Developmental Phases

Ingredient	Phase 1 Indistinct	Phase 2 Initiation	Phase 3 Illumination	Phase 4 Insight	Phase 5 Inspirational
	Safety is almost nonexistent and is indistinguishable as a core function in the organization.	Safety is based primarily on rules and regulations and is in its infancy stage.	Safety is considered an organizational objective and there is knowledge about the benefits of safety.	Safety can always be improved and there is a solid understanding of the safety function.	Safety is exceptional and the system is moving in the right direction.
	Safety Acuity: 20/180 Nearly blind	Safety Acuity: 20/80 Corrective lenses needed	Safety Acuity: 20/20 Average eyesight	Safety Acuity: 20/10 Better than average	Safety Acuity: 20/2 Hawk eye
11. Influence	If people are your most important asset, then why are they not treated as such?	Senior management provides the necessary resources for safety incentives.	Meaningful rewards are given to employees who make safety suggestions.	The organization celebrates safety achievement and success. Employees "caught being safe" are given praise and/or small rewards.	Employees are duly recognized for their safety achievements and rewarded.
12. Indicate	Safety performance is not measured very well, if at all. Senior management has no idea of the health status of the safety function in the organization.	The organization realizes if it cannot manage safety, then it does not measure performance. Measuring alone will not produce results. Action is required at his stage.	Safety metrics are developed for the organization. The organization is moving from reactive to proactive prevention and on the path to a healthy safety system.	Senior management reviews the safety management system regularly. The organization benchmarks safety performance against others in the industry.	The safety data demonstrates that the safety management system is effective. Continual improvement of the safety process has led to the organizations enhanced safety performance and efficiency benefits, such as, cost reductions and improved production output.

Chapter 4

What is a Safety Management System?

Insanity is doing the same thing over and over and expecting a different result.
—ALBERT EINSTEIN

Figure 2

A safety management system is part of a risk management strategy designed to decrease the incidence of injury and illness in an employer's operation and to address changing legislation. An SMS helps establish a framework to move beyond regulatory compliance, improves employee morale, enhances public image, and reduces employee turnover.

There are many excellent safety management systems to model. The problem is, though, that no one seems to agree on how best to find the middle ground—the balance—between a world-class safety system and meeting business and production requirements. Safety management systems are most effective when they seek that middle ground.

Dan Petersen, an icon of safety, believed that there was no one right way to achieve safety in an organization. He also believed that the safety system should fit the culture of the organization. Based on my personal experience and research, Mr. Petersen is spot-on with his belief. Every organization's culture is unique, and so a safety management system should fit the organization.

An SMS provides for continuous improvement because safety has no quitting time. Regulatory compliance is only a small part of the safety equation. An effective SMS moves beyond regulatory compliance and is tailored to the culture of your company. It is designed to decrease the incidence of injury and illness in an employer's operation and to address changing legislation.

A number of factors should be considered in implementing a safety management system:

- All aspects of the system must be clearly defined.
- Processes and outcomes must be tracked and reported. As the old adage says, "what gets measured gets done."
- Achievement must be recognized with appropriate rewards and incentives.
- All levels of management must be held accountable in the system and there should be an element of continuous improvement.
- The ingredients in the system must be statistically reliable based on easily attainable data. Safety inspections and audits are very effective in ensuring accountability. Inspection data

> **A safety management system** improves employees' attitudes toward safety, increases cooperation, creates a safety-minded culture, raises awareness, and improves communication between employees and management.

is an immediate measure of current safety performance.

What is the difference between a safety system and a safety program? A safety program can result in a "paper safety system," in which the safety program is written but never really fully integrated into the workplace. The safety book sits on the shelf—collects dust—and is never implemented. It's never maintained and it does not become part of the culture. Even when carried out conscientiously, normal safety programs may not produce the wanted results.[19]

If your company's Safety Management System…

- lacks vision or a mission statement
- is *not* properly funded
- does *not* cover safety in new hire orientation
- lacks open communication
- runs ineffective safety committee meetings
- has inadequate training or no training plan
- has no safety inspection policy
- does *not* conduct thorough incident investigations
- has no recognition plan
- has no accountability policy
- has no discipline procedures
- has no meaningful measurement tools

---

[19] Grimaldi, John V., Ph.D., P.E., CSP and Rollin H. Simonds, Ph.D., "Safety Management, 5th ed." American Society of Safety Engineers, (1989): 86.

...then you do *not* have a Safety Management System.

In order for a safety management system to effectively function, senior management must understand and appreciate the role and effort of the safety professional. The safety professional may be technically savvy, but without the people side and business side, he or she is doomed to fail. The people side of safety involves interactions with all levels of the organization. Effectively communicating up and down the organization, to the board room and to employees in the lunch room, is how safety is accomplished. To be a well-rounded safety professional, you must also keep an eye on the business-side of things, always aware of the bottom-line. I have worked in organizations in which senior management chose not to value the safety function. I have found that organizations that place profits over people usually have a high experience modification rating[20] and high workers' compensation expense.

> ### PEARLS OF WISDOM
> ✓ Creating a safety management system is not difficult—it is a step-by-step process.
>
> ✓ Regulatory compliance is the foundation of a safety management system.
>
> ✓ Continuous improvement is the key to having a sustainable safety management system.
>
> ✓ Leadership drives the safety management system.

There is value in creating a safety management system. It is sometimes difficult for safety professionals to keep their eyes on so many

---

[20] An experience modification rating is designed to measure whether your company's workers' compensation losses (also known as "experience") are better or worse than expected. If the experience is worse than expected, you are "punished" with a high mod (greater than 1.0) and you pay more for workers compensation insurance. If the experience is better than expected, you are "rewarded" with a low mod (less than 1.0) and you pay less for your workers' compensation insurance. A mod of 1.0 is average. Coomer, Timothy L. "Master Your Workers' Comp Modifier." (2003):1.

different things at the same time. The safety professional's primary obligation is the prevention of incidents that cause harm to people, property, product, or the environment. Today the safety professional must not only be technically savvy to drive the safety function but at the same time develop the necessary skills to navigate an intricate organizational environment. It's much like juggling eggs and making sure none are broken or dropped. This is where an effective SMS can help.

The basic definition of a system is "a group of interacting, interrelated, or interdependent elements forming a complex whole."[21] Safety is typically defined as "the absence of accidents and incidents." I was taught in business school that management was "the process of controlling, leading, organizing, and planning." Therefore my definition of a safety management system is as follows: A safety management system is a group of interacting, interrelated, and interdependent ingredients that form an intricate whole, which, when managed properly and over time, will significantly reduce the number of incidents an organization will experience.

While creating a safety management system may be a one-time event—maintaining and improving the system is continuous and requires a commitment of time and resources. Safety does come at a price. The commitment to safety must be supported by appropriate resourcing - of technology and equipment, training and expertise, policies and systems that promote operational safety. This commitment to safety must be consistent and visible regardless of any internal or external financial pressures facing the organization. Once the organization commits to providing the necessary resources to start and maintain the SMS that is when they can begin creating the safety system that fits their organization.

---

[21] "The Free Dictionary by Farlex." http://www.thefreedictionary.com/. Retrieved July 29, 2013.

Creating an effective and sustainable SMS is not some arcane procedure; it is simply a step-by-step process. To get started, a company must create or invent the system. The company should assess the existing culture and identify gaps and areas for improvement. Managers should write a safety policy that outlines responsibilities of the company, the supervisors, and the employees. Next, job hazard analysis (JHA), also known as job safety analysis (JSA), should be created. According to James E. Roughton and Nathan Crutchfield in their book, *Job Hazard Analysis: A Guide for Voluntary Compliance and Beyond,* the definition of a job hazard analysis is: "The focal point of understanding the complexity and interactions of a job. A technique that is used to focus on job steps and/or tasks as a way to help identify hazards before they occur." [22] It makes good business sense to understand, document and minimize the risks associated with employees performing the job tasks.

As stated earlier, the company must also be willing to allocate the necessary resources to the SMS and invest in the system. The amount of time, money, and concern senior management gives to safety is relative to the success of the safety system. An effective SMS that endures will protect both your workers and your bottom line. A company that cannot afford safety certainly cannot afford to be in business. A company gets the level of safety it deserves based on the level of investment.

The next step is to ensure that new hires receive timely safety information. New employees must know the safety expectations of their employer on day one. Employees must understand that safety is just as important as production, quality, and other company core values. The company has a responsibility to clearly communicate to employees in a meaningful way not just how to do their job, but how to do the job safely. Employees must be taught how to do their job safely before

---

[22] Roughton, James E. and Nathan Crutchfield. Job Hazard Analysis: A Guide for Voluntary Compliance and Beyond. Oxford, UK:Butterworth-Heinemann. (2008).

they work alone. In order to establish trust with employees, managers must form a partnership if they truly want to enhance health and safety in the organization. Engaged employees are one of the pillars of an effective safety management system. One of the best ways to get employees involved in the safety system is to have them serve on the company's worker/management safety committee.

Inspect the workplace regularly to find potential hazards and implement controls immediately when you discover hazards. Document those inspections and share the results with all employees. When accidents and incidents happen—and they will—conduct an investigation to determine the root cause. Clearly understand why the incident occurred so it can be prevented from occurring in the future. Also investigate near-miss incidents. It is cost effective to investigate a close call before it becomes a serious incident. And remember to seek out the facts and do not place blame. Placing blame is the quickest way to destroy your safety system. However, when necessary, ensure that your safety system holds people who fail to follow established safety rules and procedures accountable. Discipline is a form of respect; so respect your employees by letting them know when they have fallen off the track. Remember to audit your SMS at least once every year. When implemented correctly, a balanced safety incentive program can bring fun to the system and recognize those individuals who have had safety success. And, finally, you must evaluate and monitor your SMS. You must be able to measure success. Develop safety metrics that will help improve the safety system.

Whether it is ISO 18001, the ANSI Z-10 2012 system, OSHA's Voluntary Protection Program, or any number of other safety management systems available, there is no one-size-fits-all approach or quick fixes to creating a successful safety management system. As such, leaders of each company must evaluate their business as a unique community, assessing needs on a case-by-case basis to ensure accurate and effective solutions.

Through the use of an SMS, a company can drastically reduce workplace risk, in turn reducing insurance costs and the possibility of costly workplace-related lawsuits. When companies make an investment in safety, allow for everyone to be involved in the safety process, and believe internally that safety is good for the organization, it is at that point, when these companies will see an increase in productivity and profitability due to improved employee morale.

The true success of your SMS does not center on written policies and procedures sitting in a pretty binder on a shelf. It centers on strong management commitment to health and safety and meaningful employee participation. Success is investing in employee's safety training and giving them time and resources to conduct safety inspections and correct hazards. Employees are the other set of eyes and ears you need for success. You are striving to create a reputation among workers in your organization that safety rules are strictly enforced. But the most important goal is getting all employees home to their families the same way they arrived at work—free from injury and illnesses. Or, as I am fond of saying, "We want them to go home each night with the same ten fingers and ten toes that they started the day with."

A safety management system is only effective if there is an organization-wide commitment to planned processes, systems, and overall accountability. The person responsible for safety in the organization must determine how to best energize and engage stakeholders at all levels, including senior management, supervisors, and employees. It's about taking action to improve the culture, communication, controls and competence throughout the organization. Again, safety is much more than just having an SMS in place. It is about leadership that will need to direct the essential actions required to create a strong and sustainable SMS. Not to overstate the obvious, it is committed leadership that will drive the success of the safety management system.

Chapter 5
Why Create a Safety Management System?

We can't solve problems by using the same kind of thinking we used when we created them.
—ALBERT EINSTEIN

So why bother implementing a safety management system?

- There were more than 4,600 work-related deaths in 2011, and millions more suffer nonfatal injuries at work every year (Bureau of Labor Statistics).
- Nearly four million Americans are injured at work each year. Employers paid $71.3 billion employer for workers' compensation in the United States in 2010 (National Academy of Social Insurance).
- OSHA's General Duty Clause states that each employer shall furnish to each employee both employment and a place of employment that are free from recognized hazards that are

causing or are likely to cause death or serious physical harm to employees.

- The large number of success stories from companies that have implemented a safety management system proves the benefits.

> The three most important reasons for adopting or improving a safety management system for any business are **ethical, legal, and financial.**

Basically there are three vital reasons for implementing an SMS for a business—these are ethical, legal, and financial. Employers and company owners are morally obligated to ensure that work activities and the workplace are safe; there are legislative requirements primarily defined by OSHA and government entities in just about every country in the world; and a substantial body of research shows that effective safety management systems can reduce direct and indirect costs associated with incidents.

We know that safety—like any other aspect of business—can be managed and that leaving safety to chance is a sure recipe for disaster. Research shows that companies that develop and institute an SMS better manage their safety program and risk. Since 1982, data suggests that companies participating in OSHA's Voluntary Protection Program (VPP) report injury and illness rates up to 52 percent below the average for other establishments in their industry. These sites typically do not start out with such low rates. Safety management systems do work.

Implementing an SMS will assist in minimizing risk to employees and others by developing good working practices to prevent incidents and work-related ill-health. Additionally, it can improve business performance and help an organization establish a responsible image within the marketplace. Lastly, implementing a safety system will assist an organization to achieve compliance with OSHA regulations and standards, while helping the organization continually improve environmental, health, and safety performance beyond regulatory (legal) requirements.

Figure 3

Another important reason to implement a system is because health and safety professionals cannot be every place at once; an SMS provides the tools to ensure health and safety are everyone's responsibility. The idea that safety for the entire company is solely the responsibility of the safety manager needs to change. Everyone in the organization must have assigned roles and responsibilities for health and safety. A company that implements an SMS demonstrates its commitment to occupational health and safety. Independent research shows that an SMS improves employees' attitudes toward safety, increases cooperation, creates a safety-minded culture, raises awareness, and improves communication between employees and management.

In California, every employer has a legal obligation to provide and maintain a safe and healthful workplace for employees, according to the California Occupational Safety and Health Act of 1973. As of

1991, a written, effective Injury and Illness Prevention (IIP) program is required for every California employer. This Injury and Illness Prevention program must be written and the procedures must be put into practice. The required elements of this program are:

- management commitment/assignment of responsibilities;
- safety communications system with employees;
- system for assuring employee compliance with safe work practices;
- scheduled inspections/evaluation system;
- accident investigation;
- procedures for correcting unsafe/unhealthy conditions;
- safety and health training and instruction; and
- recordkeeping and documentation.[23]

To appreciate the value of an SMS, one only has to review the nature and number of accidents that have occurred over the past thirty years as a direct result of poor safety management practices. Better yet, look over the past year. An accident is a failure, and you generally only need to look at the management system to find the cause. It is well documented that an SMS is a proven process and should be viewed as

---

PEARLS OF WISDOM

✔ Safety management systems do work.

✔ Safety is everyone's responsibility.

✔ A safety management system will help the organization with regulatory compliance.

✔ The person responsible for safety cannot be everywhere.

---

[23] Cal/OSHA Guide to Developing Your Workplace Injury and Illness Prevention Program with checklists for self-inspection *https://www.dir.ca.gov/dosh/dosh_publications/iipp.html*. Copyright © 2013 State of California.

a business tool that will help the organization avoid wasting time and resources on minor or irrelevant issues. Keep in mind that you will not be able to leap from the ground to the top of the building in one jump. It takes time to change the safety culture, and progress is made one step at a time. That said, once you are on top of the roof, the view is spectacular.[24]

You know your SMS is successful when members of the workforce can give examples of senior management's positive leadership and they credit management with establishing and maintaining positive safety values in the organization through personal example. Ask yourself: does your organization have a strong, effective, and sustainable safety management system?

Some of the major benefits of an SMS are as follows. First, a well-executed safety management system *helps keep your business in business.* An organization has a responsibility—a duty—to protect employees, customers, and contractors. A sound SMS will help minimize risks to all three groups.

When employees feel safe and secure, an organization will see an improvement in employee morale and an increase in productivity. An increase in productivity generally means an increase in profitability. Isn't that why a company is in business? People want to work for a company that does not have a history of injury and illness, so a company's public image is important in order to attract qualified candidates to open positions. Furthermore, a company with lots of injury and illness is likely to have a high employee turnover rate. A strong and sustainable SMS will help reduce employee turnover and assist the organization in achieving OSHA compliance.

---

[24] Miozza, Michael L. "Keep Your 'I's' Focused." *The Advisor* 12, no. 2 (January 2013): 22.

As an example, let's look at McWane, Inc., one of the world's largest manufacturers of iron water works and plumbing products and one of America's largest privately owned companies. Following McWane's rapid growth in the 1990s, it was reported that the company had an increased number of health and safety violations.[25] In 2003, a series of joint print and broadcast reports by The New York Times, PBS, and The Canadian Broadcast Corporation reported serious safety and environmental problems at McWane plants. According to the reports, there were 4,600 recorded injuries, 9 deaths, and more than 400 Occupational Safety and Health Administration violations between 1995 and 2003.[26] The media questioned whether McWane was "indifferent" to safety.

MCWANE BEFORE IMPLEMENTING A SAFETY MANAGEMENT SYSTEM:

- poor safety record
- OSHA citations
- civil sanctions from federal and state regulators
- criminal prosecutions at six facilities with jail time and substantial fines
- increased turnover and workers' compensation costs

Prior to the media reports, the company had been implementing changes to its operating practices since 2000, according to McWane's

---

[25] Dean, Kenneth and Greg Junekg. "Tyler Pipe Workers Note Change for the Better." (March 2, 2008). Tyler Telegraph. http://www.tedc.org/news_displayarticle. php?tgtid=135&page=l. Retrieved July 27, 2011.
[26] Barstow, David; Bergman, Lowell. (January 8, 2003). "At a Texas Foundry, An Indifference to Life." New York Times.

president, G. Ruffner Page.[27] Following the 2003 investigations, McWane continued to reform its safety and environmental practices, bringing on new management and implementing new safety procedures. The company replaced 90 percent of its senior management and added 125 new environmental, health and safety, and human resources positions.[28] In addition, McWane spent over $300 million on environmental protection and health and safety (EHS), and implemented a centralized EHS management system to detect environmental, and health and safety problems.[29] The company also began self-reporting oversights to authorities.[30] McWane updated its Ethics and Compliance Policy and created a training and educational program for EHS and management skills. To ensure legal compliance, the company implemented oversight mechanisms and incentive schemes, including internal and external (third party) audits and a financial incentive program for managers based upon EHS performance, an appropriate range of disciplinary actions for noncompliance, along with a confidential, twenty-four-hour phone line for reporting suspected violations and other concerns.[31]

---

[27] Dean, Kenneth and Greg Junekg. "Tyler Pipe Workers Note Change for the Better." (March 2, 2008). *Tyler Telegraph.* http://www.tedc.org/news_displayarticle. php?tgtid=135&page=l. Retrieved July 27, 2011.

[28] "A Dangerous Company Revisited," *Frontline*, PBS, (2008). http://www.pbs.org/ wgbh/pages/frontline/mcwane/etc/script.html. Retrieved July 28, 2011.

[29] Johnson, Dave. "10 essentials of McWane's culture change," *Industrial Safety & Hygiene News* (June 3, 2010). http://www.ishn.com/Articles/Cover_Story/ BNP_GUID_9-5-2006_A_10000000000000836462.

[30] Hubbard, Russel. "McWane foundry to pay almost $2 million; Company reported own environmental breaches." *Birmingham News* (May 10, 2007).

[31] G. Ruffner Page, "Letter from G. Ruffner Page to PBS and *The New York Times*," PBS (November 14, 2007). http://www.pbs.org/wgbh/pages/frontline/mcwane/ way/pageletter.pdf.

MCWANE AFTER IMPLEMENTING A SAFETY MANAGEMENT SYSTEM:

- 100 percent compliance, 100 percent of the time
- Protection of employees, the environment and the public
- Drastically reduced injury rates, days away from work, and days on job transfer/restriction

Many McWane facilities have been recognized as OSHA VPP sites. The company was able to turn around and create a strong and effective safety system, and so can you. The organization and the employees are reaping the benefits of a highly motivated management team. In short, now is a good time to put your own safety system under the magnifying glass and view it with a critical eye.

To learn more about McWane's remarkable turnaround and the company's culture of safety visit *http://www.mcwane.com/*. To understand McWane's culture before the turnaround, watch the PBS *Frontline* special called "A Dangerous Business" at *http://www.pbs.org/wgbh/pages/frontline/shows/workplace/view/*.

Chapter 6

How to Create a Safety Management System

Even if you're on the right track, you'll get run over if you just sit there.
—WILL ROGERS

So how do you integrate safety into your organization's core business processes? Developing an effective safety management system does not come easily. The effort requires careful planning and diligent preparation. For starters, you need a management champion. You will need to determine whether safety in your organization is seen as something externally imposed or internally valued.[32] You will need to define how the organization is going to change and over what time period, and name the specific goals. You certainly will need to conduct a gap analysis. A gap analysis will tell you where you are starting from and where you need to be. A wall is built one brick at a

---

[32] Duncan, Colin, General Editor and Rebecca Nigel, ed. "The Zero Index: A Path to Sustainable Safety Excellence." Ojai, California: Behavioral Science Technology (BST). 2012.

time and so must your safety management system. The bigger challenge is not creating the SMS but sustaining the system once it has been created.

A successful system requires *not* only a strong commitment within the organization, but also a dedication of company resources—including proper staffing, time, documentation, and continuous motivation. And even the strongest systems can wither into extinction if you don't make consistent efforts to keep your system flourishing.

When you have safety and health integration, safety becomes a core value along with production, sales, customer service, and quality. This is most effective when safety and health is balanced with and incorporated into the core business processes.

When you have an SMS, you will have a systematic approach to safety and health. This system can be implemented similarly to quality and environmental systems. A properly installed safety system will go beyond basic regulatory compliance. It should focus on all hazards, and it should be a formal, documented system.

There are many standards you can apply, such as the ANSI Z10-2012 or the 18001 OHSMS. Regardless of the system you use, you will need to have a process where you plan, implement your plans, train your employees, check on the results, and entice everyone to get involved.

Change in organizations is often difficult to initiate and is quite often met with resistance. It has been my experience that you will need to identify who and what are going to be the impediments to change. Yes, believe it or not, not everyone will support safety in the organization. You would think that no one would or should ever argue against compliance with the law, and yet it still happens. I have worked for companies that have taken calculated risks with employee safety. No employer should ever cut corners or play fast and loose with workplace regulations, particularly those relating to the safety and health of the workforce. Nevertheless it happens. Companies sometimes recklessly ignore safety standards.

Resistance to change in an organization is natural. Arthur Schopenhauer, a German philosopher, said, "All truth passes through three stages. First, it is ridiculed. Second, it is violently opposed. Third, it is accepted as being self-evident."[33] Creating an SMS can pass through similar stages.

Remember, safety professionals see the world through the lens of safety. And yes there is politics in safety. The truth be told, everything hasn't always been rosy in my safety career. At times there were difficult struggles, personal attacks, disagreements, and political battles that tested my resolve. In one organization, it got to the point, where I left a six-figure corporate position because I refused to be a yes-man to management.

PEARLS OF WISDOM

✓ Find a management champion to help lead the safety efforts.

✓ Dedicate company resources.

✓ Identify your roadblocks.

✓ Avoid complacency.

✓ Have fun.

The safety management system you are implementing for your company cannot be done in a silo. You will need the support of leaders

---

[33] The Quotation Page. Quotation #25832 from Laura Moncur's Motivational Quotations. Arthur Schopenhauer, German philosopher (1788 - 1860). www.quotationspage.com. Retrieved July 29, 2013.

up and down the organization and from the workforce. You will be dealing with people who are difficult and, believe it or not, even people you may not like you very much or what you stand for. Some people go to extraordinary lengths to be difficult. You will need to learn to deal with and work with these obstructionists if you are going to be successful. Always try to work shoulder to shoulder even when you don't see eye-to-eye. My best advice, and I know it is challenging, is to try *not* to take things personally.

Additionally, know that complacency is one of things that can destroy an SMS. You must continuously work at improving, updating, and auditing the system to ensure it remains fresh.

And don't forget to have fun along the way. Richard Hawk, the world's leading expert on making safety engaging, was a safety engineer in the nuclear industry and then was a safety consultant for a wide variety of industries for fifteen years. He has a website dedicated to making safety fun (http://www.makesafetyfun.com/). His theatre background enables him to make his presentations playful, exciting, and most importantly, his style is effective at creating vibrant safety cultures.

Do you need a theater background to make safety fun? Absolutely not! When my coworker Shaun and I conduct classroom portable fire extinguisher training, we greet our class in crisp white lab coats; "O Fortuna" from *Carmina Burana* blares out of speakers; and images of flames dart on the wall screen from a projector. Do we get some very strange looks? You better believe it! We both perform a variety of magic tricks throughout the training, such as producing a flaming wallet, throwing flash paper into the air, and producing lit matches out of thin air. When people answer a question correctly we toss them a candy fireball (see the connection), which starts some friendly competition to see who can collect the most fireballs. Shaun does a demonstration on how a CO_2 fire extinguisher works by mixing vinegar and baking soda. You should hear the "oohs and aahs" as the mixture foams up and then he passes the gas over lit candles to extinguish them.

The first time we conducted this class we were both amazed by the positive feedback. Participants said they thought this was going to be another boring safety class, but then they told us how much fun they had and *how much they learned*. Neither Shaun nor I have a theater background. My point is that safety does not have to be stuffy. Create fun safety classes, throw pizza parties in recognition of outstanding safety performance, and think outside the box so that safety does not become rigid and that "extra thing" we have to do.

Another example of having fun is when I conduct emergency evacuation drills. I use a smoke machine, lock exit doors, pour liquid onto the floor, and have people lie on the ground as if they had experienced a heart attack. I'll never forget the time I used a smoke machine in the main lobby during a fire drill. As the alarm was sounding and people were coming down from the second floor, talking and laughing, they encountered the smoke. Suddenly they became quite serious and quiet. Their eyes registered fear, as they actually believed the building was on fire. I know this may sound a little twisted, but I was having fun! Lesson learned. Training gets no better!

Chapter 7

The "iforSafety" Methodology

One person caring about another represents life's greatest value.
—Jim Rohn

The ability to create an effective and sustainable safety system isn't a mysterious art; it's a step-by-step-process. A review of the literature on the topics of safety culture and organizational effectiveness—reinforced by education, personal experience, and professional training—has led to my identification of twelve critical ingredients for creating an effective and sustainable safety management system. The goal is to create an "intrinsically safe" workplace.

While there are a variety of ingredients to creating a sustainable safety system, there are basic, fundamental ingredients common to every successful safety system. There is no need for you to reinvent the wheel, because the iforSafety methodology packages the key ingredients for creating an effective safety management system into an easy-to-understand and an easy-to-implement process. The following twelve ingredients have proven to most actively contribute to the success and sustainability of a safety system for any organization:

- providing leadership by **inventing** or creating the system
- **investing** in the system to demonstrate commitment
- **integrating** safety with other organizational core values such as production and quality
- **introducing** employees' to the safety management system during new hire orientation
- **involving** employees in the system to establish trust
- **informing** employees about the system by providing clear and open communication
- **instructing** employees about the expectations of the system
- **inspecting** the workplace to seek out potential hazards
- **investigating** all incidents and near misses to determine the root cause
- holding employees accountable by **intervening** whenever necessary
- **influencing** morale by providing a meaningful safety incentive program
- providing **indicators** to measure the safety system's success

These twelve ingredients—all starting with the letter *i*—hence "iforSafety"—provide an organized way to achieve safety excellence and help create an injury-free culture or climate. Open your "i's" to what can be.

This system is *not* some cookie cutter safety management system. The iforSafety methodology is a simple, systematic, multi-faceted approach for the enhancement of an existing or ineffective safety system. It is based on the Plan-Do-Check-Act model and provides the framework for a company to build and continually improve upon a safety management system that is centered on its safety policy, practices, and programs and integrated into its overall business management process. This integrated SMS ensures safety considerations become a routine part of all products, processes, and service-related business decisions. Most importantly, it is a tool to improve health and safety performance. The ingredients are all very much interdependent and can be used by organizations of all sizes and in all industries.

There is no one-size-fits-all approach or quick fixes to creating a successful safety system; as such, managers of each company must evaluate their business as a unique community, assessing needs on a case-by-case basis to ensure accurate and effective solutions. Regardless of whether a company is seeking to establish a new safety management system, repair an existing underperforming system, or simply fine-tune a basically sound system to achieve higher performance, the iforSafety methodology outlines the basic steps to address safety culture issues, which include examination of your current culture, solutions for improvement, implementation concepts, and measurement ideas. Appendix F provides a table of the twelve ingredients and one-sentence "do's and don'ts" that embody the philosophies of the iforSafety system.

To help appreciate the value of the iforsafety methodology, I like the quote attributed to Albert Einstein, "We can't solve problems by using the same kind of thinking we used when we created them." Einstein's point was that anyone's knowledge and understanding is limited to his own experience, training, education, and information sources. I bring a different perspective and new ideas to the business owner or CEO, based on my knowledge, years of experience and viewpoints.

By applying the iforsafety methodology, it can help you transform your safety culture, by using a different kind of thinking than was used when the culture was shaped.

Through the use of this methodology, businesses can drastically reduce workplace risk, in turn reducing insurance costs and the possibility of costly workplace-related lawsuits. Above all, companies will appreciate the increase in productivity and profitability of their businesses due to the confidence, comfort, and happiness of their employees. You may have heard the term "intrinsically safe" applied to a piece of equipment, but the term can also be used to describe a workplace that has implemented an effective SMS, whereby safety has become an inherent value in the organization. Does your organization have an *i* for safety?

So where do you start? Like any journey, you must start at the beginning. Let the journey of "chasing zero incidents" begin!

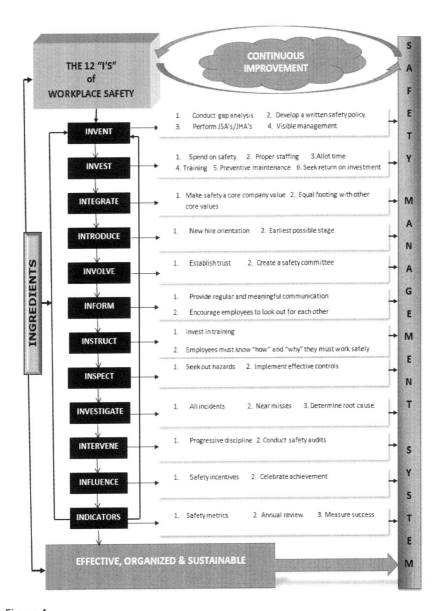

Figure 4

Chapter 8

Invent

The leader sets the organization's mission, and if this mission does not resonate deeply, then those being led will merely go through the motions.
—Srikumar S. Rao

Key Concepts: Leadership/Concern/Visibility/Vision/Innovate/
Inception/Action

This is the starting point for creating a sustainable safety system. Or, to put it another way, "this is where the rubber meets the road." The success of any system—quality, environmental, or safety—depends on the commitment from all levels and functions of an organization, but from senior management in particular. There is a Scottish proverb that sums up the message of this chapter: "He who would eat the fruit must climb the tree." The missing link in creating a sound safety management system is generally senior management oversight, so safety *must* reside at the top of the corporate food chain if the organization has any chance of reducing injuries and illness and creating a safety culture that becomes one of the company's core values. This is the stage where the vision is created. Where there is no such vision, people can perish.

> **Invent or create the safety system specific to your organization.** This is where the rubber meets the road. The actions of company leadership represent the only true measure of an organization's commitment to safety and health. Develop a safety and health policy that states that occupational health and safety is one of the company's core values.

This is the step where the planning begins. An organization can and should plan for safety because no one comes to work planning on having an accident. Senior management must set the tone and be visible advocates for safety. Safety should be planned, budgeted, and measured, like any other management system. The amount of time, money, and concern that senior management gives to safety is relative to the success of the safety system. Safety must be integrated with other core company values such as quality and production. If management believes that safety is only the job of the safety director, safety department, or the safety committee, then they have it all wrong. Senior management should consider health and safety the responsibility of all employees, including the floor or line supervisors and managers.

The inception of an SMS typically starts from something or from some event. It could be a serious accident or fatality. It could be a CEO who suddenly "gets it." It could be a CFO who sees the escalating cost of workers' compensation expense and knows something needs to be changed. It could be the safety manager who convinces senior management that safety is good for the company. It could be some serious OSHA violations. It could be a significant potential customer who feels they cannot do business with you because of the company's high experience modification rating. Maybe it stems from an employee perception survey that shows management does not truly value safety. Or maybe it's a combination of events.

Whatever the reason, the company leaders must first "invent" or create the SMS they want. Leadership must have an *i* on the future. A CEO who truly wants to see the safety culture change in the organization must be willing to allocate the resources necessary to support the new system. A health and safety mission statement signed by the CEO will tell the rest of the organization exactly what the expectations are with regards to health and safety. The statement should indicate what the company's responsibilities are, what the supervisor's responsibilities are, and what the employee's responsibilities are regarding health and safety. It does not need to be a long, rambling document—often one page will suffice. The CEO must demonstrate his or her support of the newly created system by being visible to the rest of the organization. If the CEO is invisible, the system is doomed to fail. The CEO must "walk the talk" and clearly demonstrate to all that safety is indeed valued in the organization. Safety must not be the most important value in the organization; it is integrated with other core company values. The CEO should talk about safety at staff meetings. But if he or she really wants to make an impression on the staff, then the CEO should open all meetings discussing health and safety. This will permeate and resonate throughout the entire organization.

Some ways to demonstrate this commitment to safety is by having a written safety and health policy that *clearly* states

Action Item: Integrate health and safety with other aspects of the organization.

Figure 5

expectations for both supervisors and employees, by identifying and allocating the *appropriate* resources to achieve health and safety expectations, by preparing job descriptions that *clearly* define safety and health responsibilities, by developing procedures to *evaluate* supervisors and employees safety performance, by creating methods to *correct* unsafe work practices, and by designating *competent* people to supervise employees. Remember, the intent of a safety management system is to develop a systematic management approach to the health and safety concerns of the organization.

In a survey conducted by the safety magazine *EHSToday*, over 20 percent of the nearly 1,000 safety professionals who responded, replied "no" when asked, "Does top management in your organization provide active and visible support for occupational safety and health?"[34]   Buy-in by senior management is a critical component to a valued safety and health process. The actions of an organization represent the only true measure of commitment to safety and health. Be proactive and lead by example! Often, nothing happens to improve the safety system until something bad happens. Why wait until something bad happens to reveal a safety concern and then have some government agency come in and tell you how and when to correct it?

Safety is about leadership! CEO's who are responsible to lead the organization, may *not* always understand that the safety performance of the organization is explicitly their responsibly. Leaders in an organization influence the activities, systems, and culture that produce the safety outcomes needed to drive safety performance. If you lead a company, then it is up to you—as the leader of the organization—to drive home the safety message. It is the responsibility of the safety professional to help the CEO understand the importance of their

---

[34] Smith, Sandy. "The National Safety Survey: The War between Safety and Production Continues." *EHSToday*, August 2013:30.www.ehstoday.com.

leadership in preventing injuries and the benefits of establishing and maintaining a sound safety culture.

From a regulatory compliance standpoint, OSHA expects companies to evaluate, minimize, and eliminate potential hazards to employees. It is management's responsibility to provide a workplace free from recognized hazards. Additionally, OSHA recommends that the workplace health and safety policy be stated in such a way that employees understand its importance in relationship to other organizational values.

Regulation obviously has a role in safety but use regulatory compliance as a guide, a foundation, for creating your safety management system. To have true safety success an organization must go beyond regulations.

Conduct a gap analysis in the form of a comprehensive safety audit. This is a critical first step. Please know that an audit is quite different then performing a workplace safety inspection (see chapter 15 for an explanation).

According to OSHA, a job hazard analysis is one component of the larger commitment of a safety and health management system.

SOURCE: OSHA 3071 2002 (Revised), pg. 2.

Job Hazard Analysis (JHA) is a term used interchangeably with Job Safety Analysis (JSA) and Risk Assessment. The purpose of a JHA/JSA is to ensure that the risk of each step of a task is reduced to ALARP (As Low As Reasonably Practicable). Everybody in the workforce should be involved in creating the JHA/JSA. The more minds, the more years of experience applied to analyzing the hazards in a job, the more successful the work group will be in controlling these hazards. To see a sample JSA, go to Appendix B, at the end of the book.

The value of properly written and utilized JHA/JSAs cannot be understated. James E. Roughton and Nathan Crutchfield, authors of *Job Hazard Analysis: A Guide for Voluntary Compliance and Beyond*, believe that the focal point for a successful safety management process is the job hazard analysis. Supervisors can use the findings of a job hazard analysis to eliminate and prevent hazards in their workplaces. A well written JHA is likely to result in fewer employee injuries and illnesses; safer, more effective work methods; reduced workers' compensation costs; and increased employee productivity. The analysis also can be a valuable tool for training new employees in the steps required to perform their jobs safely. For a job hazard analysis to be effective, management must demonstrate its commitment to safety and health and follow through to correct any uncontrolled hazards identified. Otherwise, management will lose credibility and employees may hesitate to go to management when dangerous conditions threaten them.

A job hazard analysis can be conducted on many jobs in your workplace. Priority should go to the following types of jobs:

- Jobs with the highest injury or illness rates.
- Jobs with the potential to cause severe or disabling injuries or illness, even if there is no history of previous accidents.
- Jobs in which one simple human error could lead to a severe accident or injury.
- Jobs that are new to your operation or have undergone changes in processes and procedures.
- Jobs complex enough to require written instructions.

How do I know this works? Charles Duhigg, the author of *The Power of Habit*, in an interview with *Fiscal Times,* stated that, "A company merely has to develop 'keystone habits'—principles or routines that can set off chain reactions within organizations—and then get the whole tribe to follow them. And then, voila, success is pretty well assured." Duhigg pointed to Alcoa and Paul O'Neill back in 1987. O'Neill needed to transform the dreadful safety record of the world's largest aluminum company when he came aboard as CEO. The day he stepped foot inside the company, nearly every plant was reporting at least one worker accident a week.

Investors thought O'Neill would focus almost entirely on profits, efficiency, and the balance sheet to turn around the company. They were astonished when he chose, instead, the company's safety record as a top priority. "Everyone deserves to leave work as safely as they arrive," said O'Neill with conviction. Duhigg told *The Fiscal Times*, "O'Neill knew worker safety was a keystone habit—a habit that can set off a chain reaction. And by changing that, he could actually transform the company."

O'Neill implemented a detailed series of measures. He installed tough new timetables for reporting employee accidents, and after soliciting input from factory workers, he enforced better employee protection measures. As the plan sunk in, employees saw that O'Neill meant business. "Alcoa's safety patterns shifted, and other aspects of the company changed as well," said Duhigg. "Rules that unions had long opposed, such as measuring individual worker productivity, were embraced." Alcoa was a top Dow Jones performer a year later. "When O'Neill retired in 2000, the company's annual net income was five times larger than before he arrived—its market cap had risen by $27 billion."[35]

In the case of Alcoa, it is quite evident that safety improvements turned into business improvements, and the company experienced extraordinary growth. This is just one example, that safety does work, and

---

[35] Mackey, Maureen. "Can Good Habits Really Mean Big $$ for Business?" *The Fiscal Times* (April 15, 2012).http://www.thefiscaltimes.com/Articles/2012/04/15/Can-Good-Habits-Really-Mean-Big-for-Business.aspx#page1.

when a healthy safety management system is implemented, it can transform a company. Anatole France, the great author, once said, "To accomplish great things we must not only act, but also dream, not only plan, but also believe." In order for the safety system to be effective, it must receive the support of senior management or it is doomed to fail. Safety cannot be viewed as, "we want to avoid opening that can of worms." Don't ever be afraid to shed light on safety in your company. Enlightened management has a core belief that safety is the right thing to do and is good business. In order for the safety management system to be a complete success, senior management must move beyond just "supporting" the system to "leading" the system. These leaders must regularly voice concern for employee safety, emphasizing it as a core company value. Once you invent the safety system, the next step is to determine the appropriate funding needed to properly implement and support the system.

SAFETY IN ACTION:

1. Crown a management champion that will lead the safety effort.

2. Create a written safety policy. It does *not* need to be longer than one page.

3. Perform a gap analysis.

4. Conduct job hazard analysis (JHAs).

5. Conduct a safety perception survey.

6. Develop self-inspections and audits.

7. Develop corrective and preventive action plans.

8. Design and implement a change management process.

9. Create written policies and procedures.

10. Include procurement and purchasing staff in the system.

11. Create a contractor management handbook.

12. Ensure that work activities that cannot be performed safely are suspended until corrective action can be initiated.

INVENT: The Leadership Stage

Who	Senior management.
What	Create a safety management system that revolves around management commitment and employee engagement.
When	This is the beginning; this is the starting point.
Why	Buy-in and visible commitment by senior management is critical to a successful system. Leaders and senior managers must do their part for safety. OSHA expects companies to evaluate, minimize, and eliminate potential hazards to employees. Additionally, OSHA recommends that the workplace health and safety policy be stated in such a way that employees understand its importance in relationship to other organizational values.
How	At this stage an organization needs to complete a gap analysis, develop a written safety policy, and perform job hazard analysis. Senior management should put a "voice" to safety.

Table 3

Chapter 9

Invest

Safety isn't expensive, it's priceless and a really sound investment.
—UNKNOWN

Key Concepts: Commitment/The Dollar and Sense of Safety/Resources

In order to create and sustain a safety management system, an organization must invest financially. It must give both time and money. Putting money into the bank earns interest, investing in stocks usually pays dividends, and putting money into the safety system earns rewards. Let's face it; accidents cost money! Investing in an SMS can pay dividends by lowering insurance

Invest in the system to demonstrate genuine commitment. Safety is good business, and a company can actually save money by spending on safety. If an organization cannot afford safety, it cannot afford to be in business! Studies show that for every dollar invested in safety, three to four dollars are saved.

expense and improving employee morale. It has been said that safety is the cheapest insurance policy. If management wants to achieve safety excellence, then they cannot afford to "pass the buck."

Workplace safety touches many other elements of an organization, including production, quality, job satisfaction, and expenses. Management commitment is the driving force behind organizing and controlling safety activities within the organization. Therefore, management must provide the necessary resources to support the safety system and it must provide the tools necessary for employees to perform their work. Stanley E. West once said, "Use the right tool for the job. Let the tool do the work. Take care of your tools." Management needs to provide the right tools in the literal sense, but it also must provide tools in the form of proper staffing, training, and preventive maintenance. If the company cannot afford safety—then it cannot afford to be in business. Besides, job health and safety is the law!

A company can actually save money by spending on safety. While the upfront cost of safety devices, personal protective equipment, training, etc. can be expensive, it is far more expensive to put the company at risk for employee injury and illness and the resulting medical expenses, lost production, fines, and lawsuits. Damaged equipment and missing parts are indicative of poor maintenance and a lack of funding that can lead to serious accidents and injuries. Studies have shown that businesses pay a high price in the long run when money is cut from safety processes.[36] An SMS will only be effective when management views a safe and healthy work environment as fundamental and applies its commitment to protect employees as strongly as its commitment to other organizational goals and strategies.

---

[36] Keller Online. J. J. Keller & Associates, Inc. (March 1, 2009).

The return on investment from running an effective SMS includes: lower insurance cost, fewer injuries and illnesses, reduction in indirect cost, and improved employee inner health. According to the findings of *The Executive Survey of Workplace Safety*, announced by the Liberty Mutual Group, 95 percent of business executives report that workplace safety has a positive impact on a company's financial performance. Of these executives, 61 percent believe their companies receive a return on investment of three dollars or more for every dollar they invest in improving workplace safety. The survey also reveals that executives realize the benefits of workplace safety go beyond their companies' bottom-line, with 70 percent reporting that protecting employees is a leading benefit of workplace safety.[37]

> **No job** is so important that the people doing that job cannot take the time to do it safely.

From a regulatory compliance standpoint, OSHA expects companies to provide employees safe, well-maintained tools and equipment. OSHA's "$afety Pays" program can help employers assess the impact of occupational injuries and illnesses on their profitability. This program uses a company's profit margin, the average costs of an injury or illness, and an indirect cost multiplier to project the amount of sales a company would need to cover those costs. The program is intended as a tool to raise awareness of how occupational injuries and illnesses can impact a company's profitability, not to provide a detailed analysis of a particular company's occupational injury and illness costs.[38]

A company should consider investing in a 5-S housekeeping program, because it has been my experience that this program is the unsung hero of both operational and safety excellence. The five S's are Sort,

---

[37] Foran, Virginia. "Executives Believe Workplace Safety Worth Investment." Cleveland, Ohio: *EHS Today* (September. 6, 2001).

[38] http://www.osha.gov/dcsp/smallbusiness/safetypays/. Retrieved July 29, 2013.

Set in order, Shine, Standardize, and Sustain. The 5-S program focuses on having visual order, organization, cleanliness, and standardization. The results you can expect from a 5-S program are: improved profitability, efficiency, service, and safety. The principles underlying a 5-S program at first appear to be simple, obvious common sense. And they are. But until the advent of 5-S programs, many businesses ignored these basic principles. Many people mistakenly believe that 5-S is just housekeeping; but it is much more than that. The principles of 5-S can be applied in any setting or application, and an organization will see safety improvements due to the removal of clutter that creates safety hazards.[39] At Milliken & Company plants, 5-S has become a foundational pillar within the company's operating system.

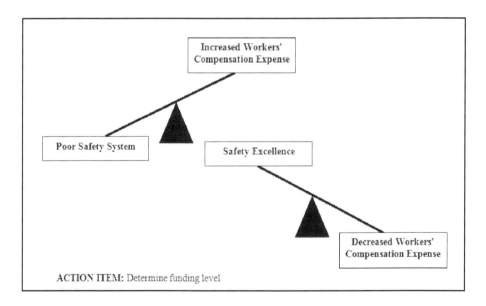

Figure 6

---

[39] Dolcemascolo, Darren. "Reliable Plant: The components of an effective 5-S program." http://www.reliableplant.com/Read/10383/effective-5s-program. Retrieved July 29, 2013.

How do I know this works? A study found in the *Journal of Safety Research* discovered that companies that provide safer workplaces for employees also tend to offer better customer service. The correlation between safety and service was found to be statistically significant. According to the researchers, worker safety brings positive business outcomes. The researchers wrote, "The results of this research bolster the business case for safety." They added that their findings, "offer good news for safety professionals because they add to the arsenal of arguments" for investing in safety improvements.[40]

The Golden Gate Bridge, connecting San Francisco to California's northern counties, had an impressive construction safety record. Joseph Strauss, the chief engineer, was concerned with the safety of his workers. In the 1930s, a rule of thumb on high-steel bridge construction projects was to expect one fatality for every $1 million in cost. By those standards, the construction safety record for the $35 million Golden Gate Bridge was impressive: only eleven construction workers died. (By contrast, twenty-eight laborers died building the neighboring San Francisco-Oakland Bay Bridge, which opened six months prior and cost $77 million in 1936, and included building the Transbay Transit Terminal).[41] Strauss made safety a high priority on the treacherous project. He made the construction site the first in America to require workers to wear hard hats, and he spent $130,000 on an innovative safety net suspended under the bridge deck. The net saved the lives of nineteen workers, who called themselves the "Halfway to Hell Club." Ten of the eleven

---

[40] BNA's SafetyNet 16, no. 3 (February 12, 2013): 17–24. The study entitled, "Does employee safety influence customer satisfaction? Evidence from the electric utility industry" can be purchased for $31.50 at http://www.sciencedirect.com/science/article/pii/S0022437512000783.

[41] The San Francisco-Oakland Bay Bridge Seismic Safety Projects website http://baybridgeinfo.org/history. Retrieved July 29, 2013.

fatalities occurred in a single accident on February 17, 1937, when a five-ton work platform broke apart from the bridge and fell through the safety net.[42]

In sports they say that a strong offense is the best defense. Well, that applies to your safety management system, too. By going on offense, through investing in the safety system, you will not need to defend against costly workers' compensation claims. You can't put a price on an accident that doesn't happen. We have discussed creating and funding the safety system with your employees. The next chapter examines integrating the safety system with other core company values.

SAFETY IN ACTION:

1. Budget for the safety system.

2. Allocate resources for time, money, people, preventive maintenance, training, personal protective equipment and safety improvements.

3. Staff properly. Watch for excessive overtime.

4. Ensure employees have the proper tools to do the job safely.

5. If the housekeeping is a concern in your organization, consider implementing a 5-S program.

---

[42] Klein, Christopher. "History in the Headlines™ —6 Things You May Not Know About the Golden Gate Bridge." (May 25, 2012). http://www.history.com/news/6-things-you-may-not-know-about-the-golden-gate-bridge.

Invest: The Commitment Stage

Who	Senior management
Who	Provide the necessary financial resources to furnish employees with a safe workplace.
When	At the beginning of the process and ongoing.
Why	There is a return on investment when an organization runs an effective safety management system. OSHA found that for every dollar invested in safety, three to four dollars are saved!
How	At this stage an organization must allocate the necessary resources to create and sustain an effective safety management system.

Table 4

Chapter 10

Integrate

In a company that truly manages by its values there is only one boss—the company's values.
—KEN BLANCHARD AND MICHAEL O'CONNER

Key Concepts: Incorporate Values/Integration

Safety is the value of caring! It is dynamic and never in a state of rest. It is affected by technology, people, processes, and priorities. Workplace safety impacts many areas of an organization, including production, quality, human resources, and finance. Safety and health must be an integral part of the business, and managers should integrate policies into their operations by involving employees in creating them. Managers must truly care about the safety of their employees if safety is to become a core company value.

In a 2013 survey of nearly 1,000 safety professionals, almost 30 percent said that safety is *not* on par with production in their organization.[43] For a safety management system to be successful, it is important to integrate safety with other organizational core values. There should never be

> **Integrate safety with other organizational core values** such as production, quality, human resources, customer service, and finance. Do not treat it is as an added activity because one core value is not more important than any other.

a war between production, other core company values and safety. Simply put, safety must go hand-in-hand with production, quality, human resources, customer service, financial and all other core company values. Do *not* treat it is as an added activity, because one core value is not more important than any other. I have worked for companies where safety exists in its own silo and has not been interconnected into the total framework of the organizational culture. It has been my experience, once silos exist, the organization does not always make the right decisions regarding safety.

When an organization states "safety is our number one priority," does this mean that safety has become a core company value? Probably not in most cases, because as we all know, priorities can easily change. During a safety meeting, ask a sales person, a truck driver, or a forklift operator what his or her number one priority is. If they just tell you something they think you want to hear, they most likely will say, "My number one priority is working safely." I would beg to differ. Their number one priority should be to make sales, deliver a load, or unload a truck. Yes, we want them to do their work as

---

[43] Smith, Sandy. "The National Safety Survey: The War between Safety and Production Continues." *EHSToday*, August 2013:30.

effectively and as quickly as possible, but just as important, we should want them to do it safely.

Turning safety into a core company value takes time and patience. But given management commitment, safety can be valued just as much as production and quality. Keep in mind that you will not be able to leap from the ground to the top of the building in one jump. It takes time to change a safety culture, and progress is made one step at a time. That said, once you are on top of the roof, the view is spectacular.

The cost savings of safe employees is well documented through re-duced insurance premiums, workers' compensation, lost time due to accidents, medical and legal expenses, and so on. But for safety to be a core value, management must truly care about the safety of its employees. Employees are the organization's most valuable assets; managers should not just care about the bottom line.

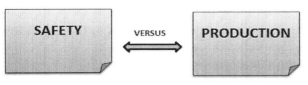

An effective safety management system requires managers to focus on safety, and not just production output, as a goal.

Figure 7

From a regula-tory compliance standpoint, OSHA expects senior management to have a written policy that makes it clear to every-one working for the organization that health and safety is important to the company. When you have full integration of safety with other core organizational values and the safety value is ingrained, the results and benefits include an improved safety culture and team environment; a healthier, safer workplace and increased morale; reduced insurance premiums and workers' compensation costs; and improved profitability.

How do I know this works? Milliken & Company is an American manufacturer that has integrated safety into its core values. Milliken is privately held and headquartered in Spartanburg, South Carolina. It is a technology-based company dedicated to building a strong culture of integrity, innovation, and excellence, and it serves the textile, chemical, and floor covering market. The magazine *EHS Today* has rated Milliken & Company as one of the safest companies in America two times (2004, 2010). The company's Safety Way approach fosters and maintains a sustainable culture of safety driven by the organization as a whole. In accepting the second award, Kevin Cox, Milliken's corporate safety manager, stated, "Milliken's safety process is driven and owned by the company's production associates and supported from the very top. Our leadership believes that safety is our number one core value and understands that the best person to tell you how to run a job safely is the person actually doing the job."[44] The company is experiencing engagement levels at an all-time high. Over the past decade, Milliken has averaged a total injury and illness rate of .63.

I suggest refraining from such grandiose proclamations as, "Safety is the most important thing we do here at ABC Company," or "Safety is priority number one." In fact, it is much more productive and responsible to just make safety an integral part of your day-to-day activities. For an organization to have any chance of experiencing safety excellence, it has been my experience that the ingredient "integrate" must be so tightly interwoven into an organization's DNA, that it is very difficult to separate the value of safety out from other core company values.

The next step in the process is to introduce the safety management system to the employees. The absolute best time is when they walk in the door the first day. The next chapter discusses setting the safety tone early and cultivating it throughout employees' tenure.

---

[44] RP News Wire. "Milliken named one of America's Safest Companies." *Reliable Plant.* http://www.reliableplant.com/Read/26861/Milliken-Americas-safest-companies. Retrieved July 29, 2013.

SAFETY IN ACTION:

1. To fully implement a safety management system, you must integrate safety into all functions of the organization. Make safety a core company value. Don't allow it to exist in its own silo.

2. Put safety on equal footing with other core company values. One core value is not more important than any other.

3. Refrain from proclaiming, "Safety is the number one priority around here!" because proclamations like this, clearly demonstrate that safety is not woven into the fabric of the organizational culture.

Integrate: The Values Stage

Who	Senior management, the safety department, supervisors, and employees.
What	Safety must be integrated with other organizational core values.
When	Start at the earliest stage possible.
Why	An organization must make it clear to all employees that health and safety is important to the company.
How	Make safety a core company value on the same level as production, quality and other core values. Senior management must write a safety policy that makes it crystal clear to everyone working in the organization that health and safety is important to the organization.

Table 5

Chapter 11

Introduce

A person's mind stretched to a new idea never goes back to its original dimensions.
—Oliver Wendell Homes

Key Concepts: Awareness/Induction/Setting Expectations

Today is the first day at work for your new employee. Getting oriented to a new job, new culture, and new people is critical for the newcomer. Safety training should begin on the employee's first day. You must start at the earliest stage possible by cultivating attitude and instilling health and safety values in employ-

> **Introduce employees to the safety management system during new-hire orientation**. Start at the earliest stage possible by cultivating attitude and instilling health and safety values in employees. Set the tone right out of the gate on how safety is viewed in your organization.

ees, even the ones with a lot of prior job experience. Make expectations clear so that employees realize right from the first day that safety is a core company value, that safety performance will be evaluated along with other aspects of job performance, and that those evaluations will affect raises, promotions, and so on.

Bringing a new employee onboard on day one with safety rules should not be overwhelming, but it should certainly always leave a lasting impression. You want to avoid information overload, because then new workers could just shut down and fail to learn more. Ensure that new hire orientation is not the only time employees are exposed to safety policies and procedures. Follow up by monitoring performance closely and asking and answering a lot of questions during those first few weeks and months to make sure the safety message comes across.

From a regulatory compliance standpoint, OSHA has no specific requirement for new hire safety orientation. But many training requirements in the OSHA standards explicitly state that training must be provided to new employees. According to the OSHA Office of Statistics, 40 percent of employees injured at work have been on the job less than one year. New hires need to be made aware of how serious safety training is right from the start. And the organization reaps benefits, because safety training for new hires is a really good and sound investment.

Introduce employees to the organization's occupational safety and health policies and procedures for the purpose of preventing work-related injuries and illnesses. Training is an important part of safety. Employees must receive training on the hazards to which they are exposed and how they can protect themselves. While training on specific hazards will vary with the job, at a minimum, all employees must receive training on emergency response—what to do in case of fire, natural disaster, or other possible emergencies.

Human resource departments typically oversee new hire orientation, with health and safety staff taking the lead role for the safety piece. Orientation aims to educate and integrate employees, not to inundate them with too much information. Make initiations interesting, varied, and fun. Involve other employees in the process; they all offer a different perspective based on their experiences. Safety education should be conducted in a memorable, non-overwhelming way. Safety training does not end on the first day; it should continue until the employee feels he or she is less like a "new kid on the block" and more like an "old hand on the job."

So what do you want brand-new employees to learn in their first few hours with their new company? Safety programs will vary from organization to organization. The most successful programs are formal, required, and include among their core information these ten must-haves:

1. basic safety policies and rules;

2. emergency procedures and equipment (evacuation routes, fire alarms, eyewash stations, safety showers, first-aid kits, portable fire extinguishers, etc.);

3. job/work area hazards;

4. required personal protective equipment (PPE);

5. hazard reporting;

6. where to go with safety questions and/or problems;

7. safety responsibilities;

8. required safety training;

9. standard safety and health information (safety signs, color-coded warnings, labels, Material Safety Data Sheets (MSDSs), etc.); and

10. housekeeping duties.

So can a company hire only safe workers? In her book, *Safety Rules! How to Build a Team that Will Drive Profits Up and Accidents Down*, Annette Estes, a Certified Professional Behavioral and Values Analyst, talks about using DISC® assessments to make better hiring decisions. The DISC® assessment is a behavior assessment tool based on the DISC® theory of psychologist William Marston. Marston's theory centers around four different personality traits: dominance, inducement, submission, and compliance. This theory was then developed into a personality assessment tool (personality profile test) by industrial psychologist Walter Vernon Clarke (July 26, 1905–January 1, 1978). John Geier, who simplified the test for better, more concise results, developed the version used today from the original assessment.[45] While I have personal experience using DISC® in one organization where I worked, I have never been involved in using it for screening applicants to determine if they were a good fit

---

[45] From Wikipedia, the free encyclopedia. *http://en.wikipedia.org/wiki/DISC_assessment.*

Dominance—relating to control, power and assertiveness
(Note: Sometimes the word Drive is used in place of Dominance)

Inducement—relating to social situations and communication
(Note: Sometimes the word Influence is used in place of Inducement)

Submission—relating to patience, persistence, and thoughtfulness
(Note: Sometimes the word Steadiness is used in place of Submission)

Compliance—relating to structure and organization
(Note: Sometimes the words Caution or Conscientiousness are used in place of Compliance)

for the company as far as safety performance. I will say that DISC®
did enlighten me to my personality traits and those of my colleagues,
and I saw the value in the assessment. Based on that experience, I
would submit that DISC® assessments may be a useful employment
screening tool for hiring safer workers.

How do I know this works? EnPro Industries Inc. is a two-time America's Safest Company winner with *EHS Today*. EnPro found that when
employees are properly trained and looking out for each other, accidents are prevented.

> "Safety is a core value. We recognize that all injuries are preventable and our motivation is our genuine caring about the
> well-being of others," says CEO Steve Macadam. Every new
> year begins with Safety First. At the start of every new year,
> employees are asked to sign this pledge: "I pledge to personally be involved to create an injury-free workplace. My dedication to creating a safe workplace free of all injuries will be
> absolute and clear through my actions."
>
> The pledge is part of the company's Safety First event. On the
> first business day of the year and prior to any work startup,
> all operations conduct a four-hour long event that includes
> not only the new safety pledge, but highlights management's
> commitment to safe production, safety training and a review
> of activities throughout the organization to focus on the importance of safety.
>
> "We have had a lot of success and created a passion with
> our proven safety practices because our focus has been
> at a cultural level," says Joe Wheatley, director of risk management and EHS affairs. "Every employee in the company
> participates in a safety pledge to renew their personal and

public commitments toward safety. We spend a tremendous amount of energy across the company recognizing the positive accomplishments and safety ethic of our employees. We constantly look for ways to increase our safety awareness, and every new employee is immediately introduced to our high safety ethic." Safety, he adds, "makes for a great place to work."[46]

Unfortunately there are many tragic examples of employees dying on the very first day at the job. Introducing safety at the earliest possible time sets expectations right out of the starting block. You only have one shot to make a meaningful first impression about safety to the new employee. The best opportunity is during new hire orientation.

The next chapter explains why establishing trust and developing meaningful partnerships with your employees is the only tried and true way an organization can enhance health and safety.

---

[46] Smith, Sandy and Laura Walter. "EnPro Industries is named an America's Safest Company Winner." Cleveland, Ohio: EHS Today (October 31, 2011).

SAFETY IN ACTION:

1. Include safety in new hire orientation.

2. Do *not* overwhelm new hires.

3. Make safety expectations clear.

4. Provide safety training.

5. Ensure open communication.

6. Review safe work procedures and other documented safety policies.

7. Do *not* forget to include emergency evacuations procedures.

8. Monitor employee performance closely during the first few weeks.

Introduce: The Awareness Stage

Who	Senior management, the safety department, new hires, supervisors, and employees.
What	To instill health and safety values into new employees on the first day of employment.
When	Start at the earliest stage possible.
Why	Employees must know what the company expects and that safety is a core company value.
How	At this stage an organization has an obligation to ensure new employees understand that health and safety is important to the company. Initiating new employees must include a safety component.

Table 6

Chapter 12

Involve

Without involvement, there is no commitment. Mark it down, asterisk it, circle it, underline it. No involvement, no commitment.
—STEPHEN R. COVEY

Key Concepts: Trust/Inclusion/Engaged Employees/Partnership/ Interaction/Shared Commitment and Responsibility/ Relationships/ Ownership/Empowerment/ Company-wide Participation

An old Chinese proverb states: "Tell me and I'll forget, show me and I may remember, involve me and I'll understand." When developing your safety culture, you need to view your organization as a community. An organization can only enhance safety and health through partnerships. A safer workplace is everybody's job! Employees often view safety as management's responsibility, not theirs, and all they have to do is follow the rules. Nothing could be further from the truth. Without employee involvement and cooperation, management alone can't successfully ensure workplace safety and protect employees. It is clear that management commitment and employee involvement complement one another. Always listen to employee suggestions, because often they provide the best and easiest solution to a safety concern.

Everyone has an important role to play in recognizing and controlling unsafe work conditions. Getting employees involved in safety is a key ingredient for maintaining an effective safety management system. A safe and healthy workplace requires each worker's active participation in identifying potential hazards. Why does employee engagement matter? Because when employees are not directly involved in the safety

Involve employees in the safety system to establish trust, because the only true way an organization can enhance health and safety is through partnerships. Simply put, safety cannot be managed effectively unless employees are directly involved in the day-to-day efforts to keep the facility or construction site safe. Real culture change in an organization comes when employees and management work together to create a safe working environment.

system, it is doomed to fail. Silos must be removed because a "we versus them" mentality just won't work. Simply stated, there is no SMS without employee involvement. No one knows the job better than the person doing it. Engaged employees are safer, healthier, and happier at work, and their performance can save organizations money on insurance cost, lost time, turnover, and lost productivity.

Relationships between management and employees are so important in safety. **Building trust** is the key element.

Employees should see safety as interesting, energizing, and practical. One of the best ways to get employees involved in the safety management process is to create a combination management and worker safety committee. The primary purpose of a safety committee is to bring workers and management together in a non-adversarial cooperative effort to promote safety and health in the workplace. An effective safety committee can assist the employer in making the workplace safer.

While OSHA does not make safety committees mandatory, OSHA does place a high value on them. The reason behind safety committees is to involve workers in discussions about health and safety on the job. It's not only a smart thing to do, but also a good business practice to include a safety committee as part of your safety system. A safety committee is a simple, affordable way to stay out of legal trouble and enlist employee buy-in with your safety efforts. As you invest in your employees' safety education, you reduce the risk of OSHA citations, fines, and workers' compensation expense. Just be sure your safety meetings are really worth everyone's time.

A safety committee can extend your reach. The committee can be an extension of the safety, human resource, or business professional. This committee can help with hazard identification, incident investigation, review and update of safety programs and safe work practices, and more. The makeup of the committee may be determined by several factors, but it should include a balance of both shop floor and management representatives (and don't forget second- and third-shift employees). The committee must meet formally regularly (usually at least once a month, sometimes biweekly, and in office environments quarterly), schedule inspections, be trained in the committee requirements, and participate in incident investigations. Often, safety committees review safety suggestions and make recommendations for corrective action to management. Just be sure your employees do not turn into the "safety police," because it can and will be a turnoff to other employees who are not on the safety committee.

When designed and implemented correctly, safety committees are incredibly effective at helping companies reduce workplace incidents,

injuries, and fines. Safety committee members can be a strong "right hand" to supervisors. Provide employees with the knowledge, skills, and ability to contribute to the goals of the safety committee. Be sure the safety committee understands its mission and that the team under- stands what resources and tools it has to get its job done. In any compa- ny where I managed health and safety, I al-

> **Workplace health and safety committees** bring workers and man-agers together to promote safety and health and resolve safety problems. They are required in several U.S. states and across Canada.

ways developed a safety committee charter to help guide the safety committee activities (see Appendix C for a sample safety committee charter document).

Safety committee meeting minutes should never be sanitized. There is no quicker way to turn people off to safety than for them to know that managers merely communicate what they want employees to know, by only sharing the good safety items that were accomplished. I once served on a safety committee where the committee chair would document in the safety committee minutes only the positive outcomes the safety committee or management accomplished. In time, both the safety committee members and the hourly workers became disillusioned with the safety committee. Members no longer wanted to serve and no one was interested in joining and serving on a committee that was viewed as a façade.

Recognize the members who serve on the company's safety com-mittee and make them feel special. Simply bringing cookies to the meeting goes a long way. Individual recognition for each commit-tee member at a company function is an important factor in making someone feel special. Unfortunately, most people are not motivated by pure altruism. Remember that most of us listen to radio station WIIFM (What's In It For Me). We want to know—what is the benefit of me participating on the safety committee? The challenge for the safety committee chair is to make sure people understand the purpose and benefits for the safety committee.

People should be recognized for their service and contribution. Post safety committee member names prominently in their respective departments. And if you want to go the extra step, give them badges identifying them as safety committee members. When others see this treatment, they are much more likely to volunteer to participate on a safety committee. Additionally, you may find it hard to rotate members because they are treated so well that they will not want to leave.

Safety is no little job! When senior management is actively involved and employees are included in the safety management system, organizations may not only see a drop in injuries and illnesses, but they will see drops in insurance costs, lost work days, employee turnover, and property and product damage. You will gain employee trust through your actions, not just your words.

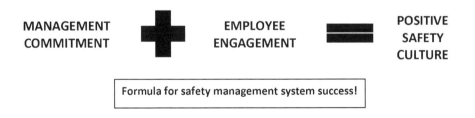

| MANAGEMENT COMMITMENT | **+** | EMPLOYEE ENGAGEMENT | **=** | POSITIVE SAFETY CULTURE |

Formula for safety management system success!

Figure 8

There are two sides to safety: the technical side and the people side. From a regulatory compliance standpoint, OSHA expects employers to involve employees in decisions that affect their health and safety. Simply put, safety cannot be managed effectively unless employees are directly involved in the day-to-day efforts to keep the facility or construction site safe. President Dwight Eisenhower said that true leadership involves "getting people to do what you want them to do… because *they* want to." Gain employee cooperation by asking them for their input and by finding solutions to safety problems together.

> Employee engagement isn't **something that just happens** on its own. It must be nurtured and developed. And it all starts with the leader-employee connection.

What can happen when you don't involve employees? Well, consider the court case of *Moebius vs. General Motors Corp. (GMC).*[47] Ms. Mary Moebius was an employee at GMC, where she operated automated spray paint guns. There was a pull cord that immediately shut down the machinery when there was a clogged nozzle. A supervisor changed the procedure so there was a five-second delay between when the cord was pulled and when the machinery stopped.

The problem was that the supervisor didn't inform or involve the workers. Mary pulled the cord and by habit immediately stuck her hand into the paint area. Due to the five-second delay, the machine spindles hadn't stopped yet and nearly took off her hand. GMC said the hazard was obvious and Mary was a veteran who should've known better than to stick her hand into a moving machine. GMC asked that the case be dismissed.

The result was that the judge sent the case to trial and GMC was faced with either offering a hefty out-of-court settlement or taking its chances before a sympathetic jury. The lesson learned is that no safety hazard is too obvious to involve employees.

---

[47] Moebius v. Gen. Motors Corp., 2002-Ohio-3918.

Safety professionals should be advisors to the organization much like the legal and human resource department. The SMS is a shared responsibility and not owned by the safety professional. I absolutely hate it when I hear, "It's the safety person's job to run the safety meetings, conduct the safety inspections, or complete the incident investigation report." I have found that the SMS is so much more effective when the employees have a voice, have a role in the process.

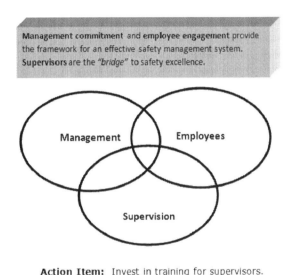

Management commitment and employee engagement provide the framework for an effective safety management system. Supervisors are the *"bridge"* to safety excellence.

Action Item: Invest in training for supervisors.

Figure 9

Getting employees more involved takes some time in the beginning, in part because we are all just so busy we don't have time to take on anything else. (That's why we try to get the safety person to do it). Once you do, however, the interest builds. And before you know it, you have a glut of volunteers wanting to help build a strong, profound safety culture.

How do you get your employees to be more invested and participate in the safety system? Here are my seven best ideas for getting employees involved in the safety system:

1. **Emergency Response**—Almost every company has a written emergency response plan. Many companies haven't tested the

plan out with a drill, or they don't do drills very often, because of the time it takes to plan and evaluate a drill. Create a small group of employees to take on this task. Use your safety committee members. I'll bet you have some employees who participate in the local fire response or paramedic service in their communities. They volunteer for this kind of task in their free time because they are passionate about it. So harness that. They may need some additional training in understanding emergency response and drill planning, and they will need to start out slow with a simple evacuation drill, but in time they will quickly become experts.

2. **First Aid**—If you are more than four minutes away from a medical provider, you may be required to provide first aid to your employees. A hands-on, instructor-led first aid and CPR class can bring employees from different departments together. Proper first aid training not only satisfies OSHA requirements, but also fosters good will among employees who recognize and appreciate the care and resources that their company expends to provide a safe and healthy environment for its workforce.

3. **Incident Investigations**—One reason we don't spend enough time investigating incidents (of all types—including near misses and property damage) is because we don't have enough time. But if you trained a small team of employee investigators to help out, you could get investigations done faster and at a level of depth that would really help the organization identify root causes for corrective action. Use your safety committee members.

4. **Job Hazard Analysis** (JHA)—Who knows the job better than the worker who is doing it? Everyone involved in implementing a job or task should be present when the JHA is written! Understanding every job step is very important. Remember, the key reasons for completing a JHA are to encourage teamwork (especially with new

employees), to involve everyone performing the job in the process, and to elevate awareness.

5. **Portable Fire Extinguishers**—Almost all organizations have portable fire extinguishers hanging on the walls. Just how important are portable fire extinguishers to business? It turns out they are *very important!* Often ignored, these overlooked life-safety devices play a vital role in keeping us safe. According to the National Fire Protection Association (NFPA), U.S. fire departments respond to an estimated 1.5 billion fires annually. These fires result in fatalities, fire injuries, and billions of dollars in direct property loss. Of these fires, over one hundred thousand were responded to in commercial or municipal buildings. Portable fire extinguishers play a crucial role in protecting property and life. Train everyone how to use portable fire extinguishers, because it is a skill that can be used at home as well as at work.

6. **Safety Committees**—If you don't have a safety committee, why not? In some states and across Canada it is a legal requirement. A worker/management safety committee allows employees and managers to jointly address critical safety issues within your organization. Additionally, this joint committee should be promoting health and safety in the workplace. Building relationships and trust between management and employees is so important in safety and a key element to success. Also consider creating a separate wellness committee as another way for employees to become involved.

7. **Safety Inspections**—Whoever does your organization's regular worksite safety inspections ought to ask at least one floor employee to help every time. Not only do you get a fresh set of eyes on the area being inspected, but you also show the employee that you think that worker has information and knowledge worth

sharing. Those organizations that are willing to pay attention to employees, and value that employees know the jobs best, are the organizations that will have the most safety success.

Hopefully these seven ideas will serve as jumping-off points that you can use to address the unique needs of your organization and have your employees become totally engaged in your safety management system. There is a safety-related poem that had a profound impact on my career and I feel the poem brings clarity to the concept of employee engagement. It's called "I Chose to Look the Other Way"[48] and tells a story about a person witnessing a safety infraction. This person who spotted the safety infraction felt uncomfortable addressing it and subsequently did nothing, and the person not working safely ended up dying. The poem goes on to talk about the guilt this person had when he saw the dead worker's wife. But the main premise of the poem, in my view, and the premise that had such a powerful impact on my career as a safety professional, is that we are all in the "safety boat" together, and as an organization, we *all* need to look out for each other. This person didn't, and someone died. The only way to ensure that we feel conformable looking out for each other is to develop and nurture employee engagement, which in turn establishes trust.

In his book, *Coaching for Improved Work Performance*, Ferdinand F. Fournies asked managers what they really want from their subordinates, and they invariably answered *involvement*. He adds that the way to get employee involvement, and the only way to know whether or not you have it, is to *make sounds come out of their mouths*. The sounds that come out of their mouths had to be in their head.[49] Wow, how simple and profound is this rational!

---

[48] Don Merrell©. don.merrell@simplot.com www.safetcal.com.
[49] Fournies, Ferdinand F. "Coaching for Improved Work Performance." Blue Ridge Summit, PA: Liberty House (1987): 83.

How do I know this works? In 2005, the Secretary of Defense tasked the Department of Defense (DoD) with reducing the number of occupational injuries and illnesses at all four hundred DoD installations nationwide. DoD selected OSHA's Voluntary Protection Programs (VPP) safety and health management system (SHMS) model to help them accomplish this task. In 2005, Air Force Base (Altus) in southwestern Oklahoma was listed as one of DoD's top-ten hazardous worksites, which was consistently reflected in reported high injury and illness rates. In August 2006, the base began developing a safety and health management system, which included implementing safety and health policies and practices. Almost immediately, Altus began to see a decrease in incident rates and a dramatic reduction in lost work days. Before starting the VPP process, Altus recorded 720 lost work days. Two years later, in 2008, 42 lost work days were recorded, which represents a 94 percent reduction over a two-year period. OSHA has recognized many of the DoD installations as VPP Star participants. According to Air Force Lieutenant Colonel Wade Weisman, "Base management and employees will attest that their preparation for VPP – particularly increasing employee involvement and using the OSHA Challenge tool [50] – had the greatest impact to date. I attribute this success to employees and management working together to make their work tasks safer….and as it turns out – a lot more efficient." [51]

Empower your employees to help make decisions together with management. Your employees know their jobs better than anyone else in the organization. Trusting and listening to them will get you on the path of safety excellence. As your safety management system matures, you should strive to move from "employee involvement" to "employee empowerment."

---

[50] OSHA Challenge provides interested employers and workers the opportunity to gain assistance in improving their safety and health management systems. https://www.osha.gov/dcsp/vpp/challenge.html.

[51] "Altus Air Force Base Utilizes Employee Involvement and Management Commitment to Contribute to a Successful Air Force National Partnership." http://www.osha.gov/dcsp/success_stories/partnerships/national/586_altus_success.html.

Your actions will demonstrate, more than words, your organization's commitment to health and safety. Your safety management system is only going to be as effective as your communication. The next chapter discusses effective, meaningful, and regular communication, which is more than just words.

SAFETY IN ACTION:

1. Start a partnership by creating an employee/management safety committee. Encourage employee participation. Build trust.

2. Establish and communicate the safety and health policy.

3. Establish responsibilities and authority.

4. Encourage employee participation in new work practices.

5. To encourage employee involvement, make sounds come out of their mouths. Management's' job is to "listen" to those sounds, take necessary action, and work in partnership with employees.

Involve: The Inclusion Stage

Who	Everyone in the organization.
What	An organization must involve employees in decisions that affect their health and safety.
When	At the start of the process and ongoing.
Why	Engaged employees are safer, healthier, and happier employees.
How	At this stage an organization should provide safety coaching to employees and involve employees in decisions that impact their health and safety. Make employees feel comfortable sharing their safety ideas.

Table 7

Chapter 13

Inform

When the trust account is high, communication is easy, instant, and effective.
—Stephen R. Covey

Key Concepts: Open Communication/Input/Feedback/Trust/ Listening/Information

Management must provide clear and open communication at every level of the organization. This ingredient is embedded in several other components of a safety management system, so it is one of the most important. Communication is much more than just words—the organization's safety message is also expressed in the amount of resources it provides toward health and safety, on how visible senior management is and how engaged management allows employees to be involved in the safety process. Management must provide employees with the information they need, not only to do their job, but also to do it safely. Managers should provide and seek regular feedback on safety.

One of the hallmarks of any great company is effective communication. What methodology are you going to use to *meaningfully* communicate to employees on a *regular* basis about safety and health? This cannot be the flavor of the month. What are the procedures for correcting unsafe and unhealthy conditions? Communicate—encourage meaningful dialogue—to ensure that *trust* is established.

> **Inform employees about the safety system by providing clear communication.** Communication is not just words; the organization's safety message is also expressed in the amount of resources it provides for health and safety, on how visible senior management is and how engaged management allows employees to be involved in the safety process.

Communication *must* be a two-way street. It is equally important that management is informed and seeks feedback from employees. Humans are the weakest link in any safety system. They are fallible and make mistakes. Through constant communication and setting high expectations, employees will look out for each other's safety as well as their own. This results in lower workplace injuries and illnesses.

Suggestions for communication include:

1. Corporate safety manual (safety rules and expectations)

2. Employee safety handbooks

3. Safety posters

4. Safety newsletter

5. Scoreboard for accidents

6. Safety bulletin boards

7. Safety suggestion box *

8. Documented safety training and follow-up (tool box sessions)

9. Safety communication with employees

10. Written programs

11. Safety and health training

12. Safety rules

13. Procedures for correcting unsafe/unhealthy conditions

14. Intranet

> * **WARNING!** Ensure that someone in the organization checks the safety suggestion box regularly. You don't want an employee dropping an imminent hazard suggestion in the safety suggestion box that no one sees for two or three days. If there were a serious incident and the cause was the very hazard that was identified on a piece of paper in the box, this may lead to litigation against the company.

From a regulatory compliance standpoint, OSHA expects companies to keep employees informed about relevant workplace health and safety matters. Employers are required to keep employees informed about their rights and responsibilities under the OSH Act. Additionally, employers must provide summaries of variance requests, copies of OSHA citations, OSHA form 300A when requested, copies of the OSH Act, and any rule that may apply to them.

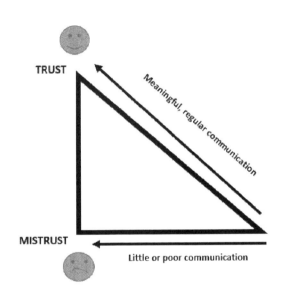

Figure 10

Documentation is a form of communication. Effective safety system documentation can help when OSHA shows up at your door. Document safety inspections and audits, document safety committee minutes, document safety infractions, document safety policies and procedures, and document all safety and health training.

An employee safety handbook is a good way to communicate safety policies and procedures. While not all inclusive, the safety handbook should provide valuable safety information to help employees integrate safety into their daily processes. These handbooks are typically distributed to new hires during initiation, and it is recommended that they read and sign for the handbook to affirm they received a copy.

Training is a form of communication. Safety training provides the requisite knowledge employees need to perform their jobs safely. It has been said that safety training is the best insurance policy against injury to persons and property. It is incumbent on the organization to fund and provide for safety training. Regular safety training allows for employee engagement, which is another key ingredient of any successful safety management system. Your organization will run the risk of jeopardizing and adversely impacting the people you employ if you do not offer essential and valuable safety training. The next chapter explains how knowledge can help prevent incidents in the workplace.

At one company where I worked, we had an environmental, health, and safety Intranet website with well over 250 documents, including policies, guidelines, procedures, blank forms, safety videos and PowerPoint trainings. There were also short training modules for supervisors called "Supervisors' Informational Series," whereby each module communicated the supervisors' responsibility for topics such as lockout/tagout, first aid, and hazard communication. This dedicated repository of centralized safety materials provided important information to employees to access any time they needed it.

How do I know this works? The EPA did a case study on AOK Auto Body, Inc., located in Philadelphia, Pennsylvania, on its health and safety strategy. The EPA discovered that because management regularly communicated the dangers of not wearing personal protective equipment, trained employees on the hazards of the chemicals they use, conducted safety training, and offered constant vigilance, AOK succeeded in keeping employees safe, healthy, and on the job.[52]

So communicate, communicate, and communicate! Allow your organization's safety actions to speak louder than your words. Open and honest communication fosters trust and leads to respect and cooperation.

---

[52] "Managing Worker Health and Safety: An Auto Refinish Shop Success Story." United States Pollution Prevention EPA 744-F-00-017 Environmental Protection and Toxics (April 2001), Agency (7406). http://www.epa.gov/dfe/pubs/auto/worker-health/healthandsafety.pdf.

SAFETY IN ACTION:

1. Communicate regularly—through words and actions.

2. Allow for feedback.

3. Encourage employees to look out for each other.

4. Build trust through meaningful communication.

5. Encourage employees to report injuries, illnesses, and near miss incidents.

6. Document, document, document!

Inform: The Communication Stage

Who	Senior management, the safety department, supervisors, and employees.
What	An organization must keep employees informed about relevant workplace health and safety matters.
When	Throughout the entire process.
Why	One of the hallmarks of any great company is effective communication. Regular and open two-way communication is the key to a healthy and safe workplace.
How	<ul><li>e-mail communications</li><li>company-wide meetings</li><li>monthly reports</li><li>safety posters</li><li>monthly, quarterly, and annual safety metrics</li></ul>

Table 8

Chapter 14

Instruct

The growth and development of people is the highest calling of leadership.
—Harvey Firestone

Key Concepts: Training/Knowledge/Expectations

Every employer has a responsibility to keep the workplace safe by preventing human error. Your employees should not learn safety by accident! Without essential safety training, you run the risk of jeopardizing your organization and negatively impacting the people you employ. Training is a large investment of finances, time, and personnel, but it is an important ingredient in creating a strong and sustainable safety management system. Consider this: Companies pay for safety training whether they budget for it or not. Failing to train an employee on lockout/tagout procedures that subsequently leads to a major accident costs the company by replacing lost wages, and paying for medical expenses and a replacement worker. For an SMS to be effective and sustainable, there must be systematic training for all employees. It should be every supervisor's goal to send workers home in one piece—and in the same condition they came to work in—with ten fingers and ten toes. Safety training helps accomplish this goal.

Another goal of safety training is to build and sustain a safety culture throughout the organization. Knowledge is the foundation of a sound and sustainable safety system; therefore it stands to reason that safety training is one of the most important ingredients of a successful and sustainable safety system.

When they are educated on safety procedures, employees will know how to prevent an incident in the workplace by properly operating machinery and handling equipment. They will also learn how to respond quickly if presented with a dangerous situation.

> **Instruct employees about the expectations of the safety system,** because knowledge is the foundation of a sound and sustainable safety system. Through proper safety training, employees must be able to demonstrate correctly the safe practices associated with their job before they work alone.

Employees should be alarmed if they see untrained workers operating machinery, equipment, or using tools. Safety training must be an integral part of a new employee's training.

A formal safety-training program is real and tangible and brings with it "lots of good will," particularly if OSHA visits the company. If you can offer assurances to the insurance company that you provide safety training to your employees, you could be offered a premium discount. Furthermore, your insurance company may be able to offer some gratis training as part of your workers compensation insurance premium.

From a regulatory compliance standpoint, OSHA expects companies to provide training required by the OSHA standards based on the exposure to certain hazards. On its website, OSHA offers a wide selection of training courses and educational programs to help broaden worker and employer knowledge on the recognition, avoidance, and prevention of safety and health hazards in workplaces. OSHA also offers training and educational materials that help businesses train their workers and comply with the Occupational Safety and Health Act. Appendix I outlines OSHA training requirements for both general industry and construction.

> It has been said that **knowledge** is the key to preventing accidents in the workplace. Look at the number of fatalities and serious injuries that occur on a daily basis. Ask yourself—if these employees had the proper knowledge—could their accident have been avoided and the fatality prevented?

It is challenging for organizations to dedicate time to training and make the training stick. Consider using e-learning. It has been my experience that online courses can be a very effective means to train. Today you can do almost everything online. You can shop, read virtual books, watch TV shows and movies, find your perfect match, Skype with relatives across town or in Italy, get an MBA, and get the training you need for your job in virtual classrooms or via e-learning. Today's learners expect education anywhere, anytime. Virtual learning allows your employees access to education without traveling long distances and without a lot of time away from work.

What's the level of safety purpose, alignment, and performance in your organization? Do people have a clear sense of where the organization is going with regards to safety and where their work fits in? Are employees committed and passionate about safety? Is the organization providing safety training regularly? In his book, *Why Employees Don't Do What They're Supposed to Do*, author Ferdinand F. Fournies says that the number one reason employees don't perform to expected standards is they don't know *why* they should. The second most common reason is they don't know *how* to do a task correctly.[53] Take a look at the conversations and relationships happening at the manager–employee level. If safety performance is not where it should be, chances are that one of these roadblocks is getting in the way.

Did you know you could get sued for lack of adequate training? In the case of Freitick v. SMS Rail Lines (No. 09-cv-1414, US District Court, Eastern District of Pennsylvania, September 17, 2010), a worker, who was not wearing work gloves when he was injured, claimed that his employer did not instruct him that wearing the leather gloves was a mandatory safety precaution. The employee filed suit against his employer, alleging that the company had violated the Federal Employers' Liability Act (FELA). He sought compensatory damages for his physical injuries, past and future medical care, past and future mental and emotional distress, loss of enjoyment of life, and past and future lost earnings. The district court denied the company's request to dismiss the claims, saying a jury should decide the matter and that there was sufficient evidence from which a jury could reasonably conclude that SMS Rail Lines was negligent for failing to define and enforce its own safety rules and for failing to properly train its employees.[54]

---

[53] Fournies, Ferdinand F. "Why Employees Don't Do What They're Supposed to Do." New York: McGraw-Hill (2007), chapters 1–2.

[54] "Did Company Adequately Train Worker on Safety Procedures?" *FosterThomas Complete HR Solutions*. Annapolis, MD (Wednesday, February 2, 2011). http://www.fosterthomas.com/hr-news/hr-news/bid/35624/Did-Company-Adequately-Train-Worker-on-Safety-Procedures.

SMS Rail Lines introduced safety-training videos for new hires, but an existing employee did not receive the same training until after he was injured. This court case demonstrates how important it is to make sure *all* employees receive proper safety training before they work alone.

By now you should recognize that safety training is a key ingredient in the prevention of work-related injuries, illnesses, and death. That being said, you may need to "spice up" your safety training to keep it fresh and interesting. To get some ideas on how to kick your safety training up a few notches, visit Richard Hawk's website, MakeSafetyFun.com.[33] Richard publishes a weekly Safety Stuff e-zine, which acts as a clearinghouse for the best ideas from thousands of safety professionals around the globe. He has authored several books on safety, including *Spice It Up! 52 Easy Ways to Turn Your Safety Meetings From Bland to Grand*, *The Safety Leader's Guide Book*, and *250 Super Bright Safety Meeting and Promotional Ideas*.[55] These resources will help make your safety training fun and interesting while still conveying the important safety message.

How do I know this works? A 2009 study entitled *Does Safety Training Reduce Work Injury in the United States?* analyzed the relationship between occupational injury rates and worker safety training. This study offered a rare look at the effects of training, benefit packages, and workplace practices on work injury. The results suggested that safety training increases the reporting of injuries but also has real safety effects on days-away-from-work injuries, especially in smaller firms. Safety training appears to be more effective in preventing severe injuries in large firms than in small ones. While overexertion injuries were resistant to safety training, toxic exposure events were

---

[55] http://www.makesafetyfun.com/.

reduced in manufacturing establishments with a formal safety-training program.[56]

How do we identify hazards in the workplace? The next chapter addresses an important ingredient in the safety management process that calls for regular workplace health and safety inspections. Not only must you regularly inspect and document those health and safety inspections, but you also must ensure that corrective and preventive action occurs. Failure to do so will be catastrophic for your safety management system.

SAFETY IN ACTION:

1. Invest in formal training.

2. Consider e-learning training as an alternative to instructor-led training.

3. Document your safety training since it may be the only proof that it occurred.

4. Ensure employees know *why* they must work safely and *how* to work safely.

5. Keep your safety training, fresh, fun and fascinating.

---

[56] Waehrer, Geetha M. and Ted R. Miller, "Does Safety Training Reduce Work Injury in the United States?" *The Ergonomics Open Journal* 2 (2009): 26–39. http://www.benthamscience.com/open/toergj/articles/V002/26TOERGJ.pdf.

Instruct: The Training Stage

Who	Supervisors, human resources, the safety department, and all affected employees.
What	An organization must train employees on the exposure to certain workplace hazards.
When	Before employees work alone.
Why	Safety training is the key in preventing workplace injuries and incidents.
How	At this stage there is an expectation that the organization will provide training that is not only required by OSHA but is also based on exposure to certain hazards. Ensure there is appropriate on-going health and safety training for employees, supervisors, and managers.

Table 9

Chapter 15

Inspect

It's not what you look at that matters, it's what you see.
—HENRY DAVID THOREAU

Key Concepts: Identify Hazards/Implement Controls/Audit

Workplace hazard recognition is the next step in the development of a safety management system. A system for hazard identification must be created, such as regular monthly safety inspections. A systematic evaluation of your safety and health state in the form of an audit is another important facet of your overall safety system. Don't wait for workplace incidents to happen before you check and inspect. Use safety inspections to engage employees in safety, because their discerning eye can sometimes spot hazards much easier and quicker than a supervisor, since they work in a specific area, or on a certain job, day-in and day-out.

Management must set the expectations, and then "inspect what they expect." Health and safety inspections aim to identify unsafe acts and unsafe conditions that may—if not addressed—cause an incident or injury. By identifying potential hazards and implementing effective controls, an organization can keep people, assets, and the environment safe.

Regular documented safety inspections can form the foundation for preventing incidents and injuries involving workers and property. Once the inspection is carried out, feedback should be provided to the department manager or supervisor. Over time, inspection reports can be reviewed to see if any trends are developing.

Hazard recognition is a proven process for continuous improvement and an excellent way to move your safety system to a higher level, regardless of what specific industry you are in. The key components of a continuous improvement process are plan, do, check, and act. Safety inspections help "check" on the system.

> **Inspect the workplace regularly to seek out potential hazards and implement effective controls.** All hazard findings must be corrected as soon as practically possible and should not be repeated on subsequent inspections. You must inspect what you expect because there is generally more than meets the eye!

So what happens when you inspect what you expect? First, people know you're paying attention, so they're more diligent. Second, you can see when motivation is slipping, and you can intervene before an incident occurs. Third, you can see which skills aren't developing fast enough, and you can re-teach them. Involve your workers and safety committee members in the regular inspections. If a hazard exists, a worker will generally find it.

From a regulatory compliance standpoint, OSHA expects companies to recognize hazards to employees and provide them a workplace that is free from those recognized hazards. Someday OSHA may want to inspect your facility or job site for a number of reasons, and you should not be frightened of this inspection. When an organization has a functioning SMS in place, managers do not have to lose sleep at night worrying about a surprise visit by an OSHA inspector. If OSHA were to knock on your company door, would you be ready? If you have instituted an SMS, you will have documentation of both regular safety inspections and corrective actions that have been initiated. Rick Kaletsky, a former OSHA compliance and health officer, wrote a very good book about the OSHA inspection process, now in its second edition. *OSHA Inspections: Preparation and Response* gives an excellent overview of how OSHA works, what employers need to do in order to have an effective safety and health program, and how they should prepare for and respond to an OSHA work-site inspection. Another good reference book now in its tenth edition, and one I think is worth having as part of your professional library, is *The OSHA Answer Book: The Employers Guide that Answers Every OSHA Question and More* by Mark Moran. One section of this book walks you through the OSHA inspection process.

I would also highly recommend supervisors attend an OSHA 30-hour course delivered by OSHA-authorized trainers. The 30-hour course is more appropriate than the shorter 10-hour course for supervisors with safety responsibilities. There are courses in Occupational Safety and Health Standards for the Construction Industry, for General Industry, for the Maritime Industry and for the Disaster Site Worker. For more information about these courses visit the Outreach Training Program https://www.osha.gov/dte/outreach/programoverview.html or contact OSHA via email at outreach@dol.gov.

As mentioned earlier, safety inspections to recognize hazards are a proven process for continuous improvement. The challenge for safety professionals and those responsible for safety is how to you get your supervisors to look for, assess, and control hazards—and bring them to everyone's attention—before someone gets hurt. Even in organizations with outstanding safety management systems, hazard recognition can be improved, because hazard management is an ongoing process, not a one-time event. Supervisors must be involved and trained in the hazard-recognition process.

When it comes to hazard recognition, even conscientious supervisors sometimes fall victim to three key oversights:

1. They sometimes neglect to recognize safety hazards because they're so familiar with their work area that they learn to work around trouble spots. At times they are so focused and busy on production output that he or she fails to see the potential safety hazards.

2. They do not control the hazard promptly because they think someone else will fix it or they'll get to it later when they are not as busy.

3. They fail to prevent the hazard from happening again. They address the immediate hazard but not the problem that caused the hazard in the first place.

Invest in supervisor training to conduct proper workplace inspections. Teach supervisors how to effectively seek out hazards. Supervisors play such an important and key role in the success of an effective safety management system. A sample safety inspection checklist is found at Appendix K.

Once hazards are identified, the organization is required to implement some type of control. There are many ways to control workplace hazards, but the preferred method recommended by most agencies, organizations, and safety professionals is to simply eliminate or substitute for the hazard. Quite often we see organizations take the easiest route to addressing a safety hazard—offering employees personal protective equipment such as safety glasses, earplugs, and back belts. While personal protective equipment offers a barrier between the hazard and the affected employee, generally this control is viewed as the least effective method to provide protection. There is a hierarchy of recommended safety and health controls found in Appendix D.

Be sure if you conduct internal safety inspections that you follow up by taking corrective action. A muffler shop in New Hampshire received a proposed OSHA penalty of $60,500 for a willful violation because the company did not correct a potential hazard. Exposed, energized wires that could cause an electric shock were left in a restroom even after their discovery through in-house safety inspections. A willful violation is one committed with intentional, knowing, or voluntary disregard for the law's requirements, or with plain indifference to worker safety and health.[57] If you recognize a safety hazard that could cause bodily injury or death you have both a moral and legal obligation to take corrective action.

It is important to understand that an inspection of the workplace is quite different from an audit of the workplace. The tools you use are similar, but the processes and how they are conducted make them quite different. An inspection generally uses a checklist format with "yes or no" answers. The question is asked, or the item on the checklist is evaluated, and it either passes the inspection or it does not. "Shades of gray" very seldom come into play during an inspection.

---

[57] "Muffler Shop Faces OSHA Fines." *Foster's Daily Democrat* (May 21, 2013). http://www.fosters.com/apps/pbcs.dll/article?AID=%2F20130521%2FG-JNEWS_01%2F130529836%2F-1%2FFOSNEWS&goback=%2Egde_1417147_member_242740603.

Inspections are usually performed in a very short timeframe (usually between ten minutes and an hour), and they usually focus on a single facility, department, item, or process.

Most organizations with successful safety systems have well-organized safety audit programs. The safety audit is much more detailed and in-depth than a safety inspection. An audit can take several hours or several days to complete, depending on the scope and depth of the audit. Audits look at an entire safety management system from start to finish, and will include reviews of written procedures and observation of tasks as well as an inspection of the equipment and processes to which the written procedures apply. Audits frequently include interviews with employees and document reviews to assure that the steps an operator actually takes are in-line with the written procedure (Do the procedures say what the operators do? And do the operators do what the procedures say?). Additionally, if a procedure is based on a regulatory requirement, an audit will evaluate a written procedure to assure it meets the requirements of the regulations. With an audit, there is frequently a question checklist that determines if the topic "meets compliance," "needs improvement," "does not meet compliance," or is "not applicable."

Audit tools will generally be more "squishy" to allow for the auditor to probe deeper into the process to determine if it complies, and to what degree it complies. Audit tools and questions are seldom in a yes/no format, and the tools are designed so that auditors ask open-ended questions that allow for the operator to elaborate on what they do and how they do it. Auditing is as much about people skills as it is about technical skills. Audit findings are generally more detailed in nature and point out specifically what is required and what parts of the process are out of compliance (hence the availability of the "needs improvement" determination).

How do I know this works? A peer-reviewed study published in *Science Magazine*, conducted by professors at the University of California and Harvard Business School, indicated that government workplace inspections save lives, reduce workers' compensation claims, and do not cost jobs.[58] It stands to reason that if government inspections are proven to save lives and reduce costs, then regular internal inspections by competent people should have the same effect or impact. The study found that within high-hazard industries in California, inspected workplaces reduced their injury claims by 9.4 percent and saved 26 percent on workers' compensation costs in the four years following the inspection, compared to a similar set of uninspected workplaces. On average, inspected firms saved an estimated $355,000 in injury claims and compensation for paid lost work over that period. What's more, there was no discernible impact on the companies' profits.[59]

A great quote from John Lubbock is, "What we see depends mainly on what we look for." Workplace safety inspections are essential to identify potential health and safety hazards. Safety audits are essential because it allows the organization to take a "deep dive" exploring the safety management system. By keeping workplace safety in sight, an organization will keep people, product, and property safe. You may regularly perform workplace inspections and audits and still have an incident! Now what? The next chapter focuses on incident and near-miss investigations and discusses why it is important that the incident investigator does not seek to place blame.

---

[58] "Randomized Government Safety Inspections Reduce Worker Injuries with No Detectable Job Loss" was co-authored by Harvard Business School Professor Michael Toffel, Professor David Levine of the Haas School of Business at the University of California, Berkeley, and doctoral student Matthew Johnson. Science Magazine Vol. 336 no. 6083 pp. 907-911 (May 18, 2012).

[59] Harvard Business School. "New Study Shows That Workplace Inspections Save Lives, Don't Destroy Jobs:
OSHA Regulations Can Be Good for Workers' Health." (May 17, 2012). http://www.hbs.edu/news/releases/Pages/toffelscience051712.aspx.

SAFETY IN ACTION:

1. Document a formal procedure to conduct inspections.

2. Conduct documented inspections on a regular basis.

3. Take corrective action as soon as possible.

4. Never allow for repeat findings.

5. Establish risk reduction/hazard control process (use the hierarchy of safety and health controls found in Appendix D).

6. Regularly audit the safety management system.

Inspect: The Prevention Stage

Who	Senior management, the safety department, supervisors, and employees.
What	An organization must recognize hazards to employees and provide them a workplace free from those recognized hazards.
When	All hazard findings must be corrected as soon as practically possible.
Why	Regular documented safety inspections can form the foundation for preventing incidents and injuries.
How	At this stage an organization should create a system that identifies hazards and implements effective controls. Conduct regular self-inspections covering the entire worksite.

Table 10

Chapter 16
Investigate

History is a vast early warning system.
—Norman Cousins

Key Concepts: Incident Investigation/Root Cause/Near Misses

"Close" only counts if you're throwing horseshoes or hand grenades, right? Well, not if you're a safety professional. Close calls are your opportunity to prevent mishaps before they cause serious injuries. Things happen! Management should thoroughly look into every incident and near-miss for the root cause. Drill down...why, why, why? Is there a flaw in our system—did we miss something? It's vital that members of an organization know about accidents, injuries, incidents, and near misses as soon as they happen so they can be prevented in the future, thereby saving lives, time, and money. Establish written procedures for investigating all workplace incidents, accidents, and illnesses, so that recommendations can be made for appropriate corrective action to prevent recurrence.

There is much debate in the literature about whether there is difference between describing a workplace safety event as an accident or an incident. An accident is often described as a random act that could not be prevented. An incident is generally described as an unplanned or undesired event that may cause injury, illness, or property damage but may have been prevented with preparation.

Quite frankly, I think safety professionals spend way too much time debating the difference between these two terms. I personally feel that the words can be used interchangeability. I can see both sides of the argument (Go figure; I'm a Libra and all about the balance). That being said, because I am not so hung up on whether we call safety events in the workplace accidents or incidents, I will lean toward calling these events "incidents," solely because the word *incident* starts with the letter "i," and that works nicely with my iforSafety management system methodology.

> **Investigate all incidents and near misses to determine the root cause, holding employees accountable**. Incident investigation and analysis is an essential ingredient of a safety management system. Most workplace incidents are preventable and each one has a cause; once identified, they can be eliminated to prevent recurrences.

We must always move past blame. Investigating incidents should always be fact-finding missions, not fault-finding missions. Most incidents are attributable to a failure in the safety management system: lack of training, failure to discipline, lack of appropriate resources, etc.

From a regulatory compliance standpoint, OSHA expects companies to conduct thorough accident investigations. An excellent resource is Jeffrey

S. Oakley's book, *Accident Investigation Techniques*. His book provides accident investigation techniques that companies, safety professionals, and those charged with the responsibility for safety can use to analyze accidents and feel assured that the causes have been properly determined and corrective actions will be initiated to prevent recurrence.

> Workplace incidents are **defects** in the safety management system.

One of the single most common causes of workplace injuries and fatalities is the "it can't happen here" attitude. No one comes to work to intentionally make a mistake that will lead to a workplace injury. But when it happens, all hell can break loose. An effective incident investigation program is one of the most powerful tools a safety professional has to identify, assess, and mitigate risk in the workplace. Yet, too often, workplace incidents are not fully or properly investigated, simply because of the huge amount of time and work involved. Unfortunately, even the most experienced supervisors are often not aware of simple, proven techniques that can immediately make it far easier to conduct effective incident investigations in far less time. Worse still, many incident investigations are conducted with ineffective, inefficient, and outdated tools and techniques. The result is incident investigations that take too much work and time, and often fail to fully identify risk or prevent further safety incidents. Over the course of my career, I have noticed that organizations often fail to invest in training supervisors on how to conduct proper incident investigations. But with proper training, supervisors' skills and assistance will be a major asset to the safety professional or person responsible for safety when a workplace incident occurs.

Incident investigation should occur in a way that reinforces the organization's desire to take care of employees and continuously improve safety by reducing exposure to hazards. Creating an incident investigation process that achieves those objectives requires pre-planning. No matter the process in place, incident investigations should all have one primary goal: the safety of the employee.

A near-miss accident or incident should serve as a wake-up call to the organization. It is less costly to investigate a near miss than a serious incident. A good investigation program will collect the facts, determine the root causes, establish controls to prevent recurrence, identify trends, and allow the organization to demonstrate commitment to the safety management system. One of the quickest ways to kill your SMS is to allow near misses that are reported to go uninvestigated. For instance, if a supervisor is told that his forklift operators are driving too fast through the warehouse and then someone from the office gets struck by one, it is too late.

> **OSHA defines a near miss as** incidents where no property was damaged and no personal injury sustained, but where, given a slight shift in time or position, damage and/or injury easily could have occurred.
>
> **Source:** OSHA website

Companies that focus on leading indicators, such as near-miss reporting, show improved organizational safety performance. According to Wikipedia, the free encyclopedia, a "near miss" is an unplanned event that did *not* result in injury, illness, or damage—but had the potential to do so. Only a fortunate break in the chain of events prevented an injury, fatality, or damage; in other words, a miss that was nonetheless very near. Sometimes in the literature near misses are referred to as "near hits." Since there is no agreed upon term and concise meaning for a near-miss incident, each organization should create its own clear definition of a near miss.

You can reduce losses resulting from incidents and injury through the investigation of your near misses. Near misses should be treated as wake-up calls that can help prevent serious incidents in the workplace. When you have a near miss in your workplace, do you feel relieved (whew, we were lucky) and then you just drop it? In my opinion, that is a *big* mistake and a *lost* opportunity. Proactively investigating and analyzing near misses can improve your safety system and prevent catastrophic incidents. Investigating near misses rather than an actual incident can save an organization some significant money and time because it is much more cost effective and easier to investigate something that did not result in a serious injury or severe property damage than an incident that did.

How do I know this works? A peer-reviewed magazine article, "Near-Miss Reporting—a Missing Link in Safety Culture," examines several studies that have shown near misses greatly outnumber serious accidents involving fatality, injury, or property damage. "We want to develop a culture that doesn't wait until someone is injured, but identifies the risk before it happens," explained the article's author Mike Williamsen, Ph.D., CSP, who added that it is important to develop a safety culture that engages all employees. "We have to engage people on the front line to eliminate personal risks."[60] Companies just cannot afford not to investigate near misses, given how they outnumber actual incidents. By identifying near misses and addressing cause, you can improve profits, and you can prevent any potential hazards threatening people or equipment.

---

[60] Smith,Sandy. "Increased Near-Miss Reporting Results in Improved Safety Performance." *EHS Today.* (May 3, 2013). Mike Williamsen, Ph.D., CSP. "Near-Miss Reporting: A Missing Link in Safety Culture." *Professional Safety* (May 2013): 46–50. *Professional Safety* is published by the American Society of Safety Engineers.

Now that you have established the foundation of a safety management system and the process is well on its way, how do you make certain that everyone is doing what needs to be done to ensure success? The next chapter deals with accountability and enforcement, which I believe are the most critical ingredients in a safety management system.

SAFETY IN ACTION:

1. Document a formal procedure to conduct incident investigations.

2. Determine incident root cause.

3. Never place blame. Investigations should be fact-finding missions.

4. Investigate near misses.

5. Train supervisors in incident investigations.

Investigate: The Root Cause Stage

Who	Safety department along with supervisors and trained employees.
What	An organization must conduct thorough incident investigations to identify, assess, and mitigate risk in the workplace.
When	Investigate incidents and near misses as they happen.
Why	Most incidents are attributable to a failure in the safety management system, so it is vital to the organization to understand the root cause so corrective action can be initiated.
How	At this stage an organization must conduct incident investigations that get to the root cause. Train your supervisors to assist.

Table 11

Chapter 17

Intervene

The single greatest safety system failure...is the lack of accountability.
—Dan Petersen

Key Concepts: Accountability/Enforcement/Prevention/Control/
Corrective Action

Does your safety system have teeth? The only way your safety management system will work is when employees follow established safety rules and regulations. Corrective action must be initiated promptly when serious safety and health hazards are discovered. People must follow established workplace safety procedures. Progressive discipline (a succession of increasingly firmer reprimands that give the employee multiple opportunities to correct undesired behavior) is a form of respect. The steps in the progressive discipline process are oral warning, written warning, suspension and termination. So if employees are not following safety procedures, they must be held accountable. However, know there is a fine balance between holding employees accountable for not following workplace procedures that lead to an incident and ensuring that an incident did not occur because of a safety system breakdown.

It must be understood that progressive discipline is a last resort for improving safety performance. Before issuing discipline, always analyze the safety management system first to ensure it is not a breakdown of the safety system. When it comes to discipline, the incident itself is irrelevant. The objective is to help the employees, not hurt them. Nevertheless, there are circumstances when corrective discipline will be required to reinforce, with some employees, that management is serious about safety. When done correctly, discipline can be a form of respect. Remember that enforcement of safety procedures and practices is a key ingredient of your organization's culture.

> **Intervene whenever necessary with progressive discipline** because people must follow established workplace safety procedures. All people in the organization must be accountable and have a clear understanding of the consequences for failing to perform their health and safety responsibilities. Discipline demonstrates that your safety system has teeth! Accountability is one of the most critical components of a safety management system.

Your SMS only works when employees follow established safety rules and regulations. When that doesn't happen, you have to correct it with employee re-training, progressive discipline, and, the choice of last resort, termination. While discipline is not pleasant, you have to do something. Failing to act when an unsafe employee ignores safety practices or engages in reckless behaviors can undermine and destroy your safety culture. Morale sinks, injury risk increases, and you face greater exposure to compliance-related complaints and citations. You may consider having your safety committee conceive, and management approve, a disciplinary action plan. Effective management of your safety system helps protect both your employees and your organization's bottom-line.

Over time, a lack of discipline for minor safety and health infractions sends a message to employees that there are no consequences for health and safety violations. If workers understand they're being judged as much for safety as they are for production, they'll be less likely to overlook the safety rules. Showing them a written discipline policy, and having them sign a contract stating that they've read and understand the policy can emphasize its importance.

From a regulatory compliance standpoint, OSHA expects companies to discipline employees who fail to adhere to established safety policies and rules. I believe that employees do not come to work to intentionally make mistakes that will cause them to get hurt. However, there are some employees who, for a variety of reasons, will not follow safety procedures. In order for your SMS to be effective, you must discipline employees who can't—or won't—follow your organization's safety rules.

Accountability links responsibility to consequences. Consequences can be negative or positive and can range from condition of employment to safety incentives. There must be balance, and actions must always be fair, consistent, timely, and relevant. Safety is about accountability. And without accountability, there is no safety.

Safety accountability is vitally important to the overall success of any safety management system. An organization that fails to demand

One of the best recipes for injury prevention is safety accountability. **What's in the recipe?** Management commitment, a written safety policy, safety system resources, employee engagement, written safety programs that outline responsibilities, measurement tools, corrective action, and positive and negative reinforcement of the safety system. Safety accountability is not about playing the blame game! It's about saving lives. And who can't enjoy that recipe?

safety accountability fails every member of the organization. When safety roles and responsibilities are assigned without follow-up on performance, it signals that the safety assignments are not truly important to the organization. What you should do is routinely check on progress and provide feedback on performance against safety-related roles and goals.

We have all heard the expression, "what gets the heat gets done." I have worked in organizations where safety accountability was quite evident, and I have worked in others were accountability was non-existent. Generally people will only perform to the level they are measured. Safety is everybody's business, and it should be a condition of employment.

The majority of the injuries that occur are not related to unsafe workplace conditions, but are connected to behavioral issues in the workplace. Real success calls for a recipe with a dash of OSHA compliance, a touch of behavioral sciences, and all placed in a safety accountability piecrust. Clear accountability for safety is the magic ingredient that is often left out of the entrée. Many people simply do not understand why workplace injuries continue despite their attempts at implementing compliance-based programs. Compliance-based safety programs are only the bare minimum a company needs to meet. An organization must go beyond mere compliance if it seriously wants a safety culture in which people look out for each other.

So, hopefully, you are asking yourself, "What does safety account-ability look like?" Consider the following for your organization:

- **Management commitment**—A significant factor in success-ful safety system development and ongoing support. Manage-ment should make it a very public commitment. See Appendix G for a Safety Policy Statement example and the other appen-dices for safety system resources.

- **Define basic expectations**—Clearly define safety expecta-tions for all personnel. What does your company expect from employees in regard to injury prevention?

- **Specific safety management responsibilities**—Once the rules are defined, leaders should have a clear understanding of what is expected of them. In order to hold people accountable for safety performance, they must clearly understand their own responsibilities.

- **Measurement**—Organizations routinely measure productivity or quality, but safety is often omitted from the annual review process. Safety is a key ingredient to business success, so goals must be set and progress tracked.

- **Recognition and corrective action**—Recognize positive and negative safety performance as you would any other re-sponsibility. Do not confuse recognition with only incentives. And remember that accountability may mean consequences, both positive and negative.

In my view, supervisors have the primary responsibly for safety account-ability, because often they are the closest to the worker. Supervisors must be firm when enforcing safety policy. If a supervisor is wishy-washy, this sends the wrong message to the offending employee. Supervisors must accept the fact that they are not in a popularity contest. When they correct or discipline employees, they are doing it for the employees' (and their families') best interest. I have always felt that discipline applied consistently and fairly was a form of respect. Telling employees that you care for their well-being and want them to continue to be part of the team shows them respect. When they get off-track, you are helping them get back on-track. What's wrong with that?

A supervisor should try to avoid being a perfectionist, because this is one characteristic that can destroy a supervisor's effectiveness. We have all heard people say that "management does not fire employees, employees fire employees," meaning that employees generally behave in such a way that they get themselves fired from the job. When super-visors have followed the company's progressive discipline policy, they should be able to fire employees without feeling guilty about it. And, lastly, supervisors should empathize with employees, but they must also find balance and maintain healthy emotional boundaries.

How do I know this works? Writing for the June 1, 2010 issue of *EHS Today*, David Maxfield noted that when companies recognize the val-ue and accountability of safety they can, "…leverage that learning to improve quality, production, cost control and customer service." Maxfield conducted a study whereby he took 420 supervisors and managers and divided them into two groups. The leaders in the first group were selected because they held their people accountable for every aspect of safety. The leaders in the second group were se-lected because they did not. He wanted to test whether there were tradeoffs between safety and other priorities or whether accountabil-ity in safety predicted success across all priorities.

The findings couldn't be more dramatic. When he compared the 20 percent of leaders who focused the most on safety to the other 80 percent, the safety-focused leaders were 5 times more likely to be in the top 20 percent on productivity, quality, efficiency, and employee satisfaction.

His data clearly demonstrated that being the best in workplace safety makes you the best in each of these other areas. And these results hold true across multiple industries, including oil and gas exploration, chemical manufacturing, power generation, and construction. Regardless of the industry, the leaders who are best at holding their people accountable for safety also achieve the best quality, productivity, and efficiency. This study shows the strategic importance of the norms, skills, and behaviors involved in accountability.[61]

Safety coaching is vitally important to safety system success. As the safety professional or the person responsible for safety, be sure you are not viewed solely as the "safety cop." The safety professional is an advisor to the organization and should be viewed more like a "safety coach" when interacting with supervisors and employees. There certainly may be times when you will need to be the safety cop, such as when you come across someone working unsafely. But more times than not, you should be viewed as a safety coach.

There must be accountability for the results of the SMS. I love this saying, "People should know what you stand for. They should also know what you won't stand for." If organizational leaders don't know what results they expect from the SMS, then they need to figure it out. Employees should know what their leaders expect. They should also know what they won't stand for.

---

[61] Maxfield, David. "Workplace Safety is the Leading Edge of a Culture of Accountability." *EHS Today.* (June 1, 2010). http://ehstoday.com/safety/news/workplace-safety-leading-edge-culture-accountability-7790.

Lastly, managers should regularly, at least annually, audit their systems (health and safety, environmental, and post-injury) against a recognized standard such as the American ANSI Z-10—2012 standard or the European ISO 18001 standard. This will tell the organization whether the safety management system is functioning properly and how the system can be improved.

On the other side of the spectrum from discipline is reward. Chapter 18 speaks to the value of safety incentives. Organizations should celebrate safety accomplishments, and individuals should be recognized for contributions to the success of the safety management system.

SAFETY IN ACTION:

1. Create a written progressive discipline policy. Ensure unacceptable safety actions are clearly defined.

2. Communicate to employees the safety rules and the penalties for *not* complying.

3. Before issuing discipline, be sure there was no breakdown in the safety management system.

4. Only when necessary, and as a last resort, use progressive discipline to hold people accountable. Use it objectively!

5. Apply discipline fairly and consistently.

6. Keep a record each time you discipline for violating a safety-related rule. Document oral warnings, as well.

7. Management should audit the safety management system at least annually.

8. Be more of a safety coach than a safety cop. You will need to be both when circumstances call for it.

Intervene: The Accountability Stage

Who	Everyone in the organization.
What	An organization must discipline employees who fail to adhere to established safety policies and rules.
When	Corrective action and progressive discipline must be initiated promptly.
Why	There are circumstances where discipline will be required to reinforce that management is serious about safety.
How	At this stage an organization must discipline employees who fail to follow established safety policies and rules through verbal warnings, corrective actions, suspensions, and possible terminations.

Table 12

Chapter 18

Influence

Pleasure in the job puts perfection in the work.
—ARISTOTLE

Key Concepts: Morale/Motivation/Incentives

The long debate about the use of safety incentives has continued into 2013. Can an organization create a positive, OSHA-friendly employee safety incentive program that will be a balanced part of its overall safety and health management system?

The simple answer is "Yes."

In a 2011 OSHA memo, David Michaels, Assistant Secretary of Labor for the Occupational Safety and Health Administration (OSHA), shared this opinion:

"A positive (safety) incentive program encourages or rewards workers for reporting injuries, illnesses, near-misses, or hazards; and/or recognizes, rewards, and thereby encourages worker involvement in the safety and health management system. Such an incentive program can be a good thing and an acceptable part of a (VPP) quality safety and health system."

> **Influence morale by providing a meaningful safety incentive program.** This is the fun part of the safety system. When implemented correctly, a safety incentive program will easily justify any expense it incurs through a reduction in the costs associated with injuries and incidents. Organizations should celebrate safety achievement and successes.

Based on Michael's statement, it appears OSHA is not totally against safety incentive programs. That being said, OSHA inspectors, senior executives, and financial people are examining what safety measures employers choose to focus on in their safety incentive program. What gets measured differs from company to company and industry to industry, but the golden rule has been set for all employee safety incentive programs: "Thou shall not appear to encourage or to promote non-reporting of illnesses or injuries."

In the end, a balanced safety incentive program will measure and recognize your people for safety engagement on and off the job. And it will, if properly structured, raise safety awareness, reduce incidents, and increase the bottom line—all without encouraging non-reporting of incidents. Supervisors should develop team safety goals, communicate the progress toward those goals, and reward results. It is wise to consider making production incentives conditional on employees following safety rules.

Safety professionals must recognize that effective safety management has always included an understanding of human resource issues. Many organizations state, "Our most important asset is the people who work for us." If people are the most important asset, then they should be treated as such. It should be an organizational goal to make sure they are safe at work. Remember that forming relationships in safety are extremely important if an organization truly wants to build a strong safety culture.

> It's easy to catch someone doing something **wrong safety-wise** and address it. It is far more difficult—but so very important—to catch someone doing something **right safety-wise** and address that behavior in a positive fashion.

Organizations that use a properly structured safety incentive program will protect against employee incidents by focusing employees on the safety culture, promote and sustain the safety culture, and, ultimately, support the process of change and strengthen the safety environment that will lower insurance and lost-time costs.

People must be motivated to perform in a certain way. Employees should be recognized for their safety achievements and rewarded, much like a sales person is recognized and rewarded for reaching a sales quota. Incentives help put a spotlight on safety, and proactive organizations reward safety observations, suggestions, and best practices. Organizations should celebrate safety achievement and successes. It is important to note that rewards must be meaningful enough to motivate employees. In one organization where I worked, the company handed out company calendars and small trinket-like calculators at the end of the year for safe work performance. Employees pooh-poohed these token gifts and felt management placed little value on their safety. The good intentions by management backfired. Rewarding safe behavior with meaningful incentives will raise company-wide awareness of safety issues, reduce injuries, and instill a proactive work ethic, therefore fostering a safer working environment.

Think about this. An employee with a positive outlook is just as infectious in improving morale in the workplace as a displeased employee is in ruining morale. It is far better to "incent" your employees, then to "infuriate" them.

From a regulatory compliance standpoint, OSHA does not expect or require companies to have safety incentives programs. OSHA may actually frown on a company that does offer such incentives, because sometimes these programs can lead to under-reporting/under-recording of injuries and illnesses. However, if the safety system is exceptional and the company can demonstrate that employees are not underreporting accidents, OSHA should be OK.

How do I know this works? South Carolina Gas, a southern electric company, once tied its safety suggestion program to a comprehensive recognition program. In the first month of the program, the utility company received five times as many suggestions as were received the entire previous year.[62]

The Department of General Services in Sacramento, California, found that a new safety recognition program motivated employees to come forward with some significant potential lifesaving suggestions.[63]

---

[62] Dandes, Rick. "Effective Safety Incentive Programs Can Help Cut Spending." Premium Incentive Products: Health, Well-Being Come First. http://www.pipmag. com/feature_print.php?fid=201009fe05. (2010).

[63] "Hazard Identification & Recognition Program." Department of General Services, Sacramento, California (2008).

Although the debate about the value of safety incentives has not been settled, the latest information does indicate that safety incentive programs offer opportunities for continuous improvement. It is important for management to determine what they intend to accomplish with an initiative and then consider the value-add *before* committing company resources.

If the organization sees the value-add, then the safety incentive program must be funded appropriately. As mentioned earlier, nothing can kill a safety incentive program quicker that giving well-compensated employees trivial rewards for working safely. The reward must be meaningful, timely, and, most importantly, fairly administered. And, lastly, the program must not be regarded as an opportunity for management to reward production and quality quotas. As the debate rages on, employees and employers alike can begin to reap the reward of implementing and participating in a well-structured safety incentive program.[64]

A safety incentive program is just one ingredient in an organization's whole safety system. If done properly, I believe a well-structured safety incentive program, which ties into the organization's broader goals, reflects continuous improvement, is properly funded and not gimmicky, and does not create a disincentive to report injuries, can and will be a valuable ingredient of a quality safety system. The literature suggests that organizations that regularly reward and recognize safety achievement and success and who have an effective safety accountability system in place seldom have to discipline their employees for safety infractions.

---

[64] Miozza, Michael L. and David C. Wyld, "The Carrot or the Soft Stick? The Perspective of American Safety Professionals on Behaviour and Incentive-Based Protection Programmes." *Management Research News* 25, no. 11 (2002).

The final ingredient in the iforSafety methodology addresses the need to measure the success of the safety management system. The next chapter is about how an organization evaluates its safety system using a combination of past, current, and indicating data. An organization cannot have an effective safety system without measurement.

SAFETY IN ACTION:

1. Provide meaningful safety incentives.

2. Recognize employees for their safety achievements and successes.

3. Make production objectives conditional on adhering to safety rules.

4. Ensure your safety incentive program is *not* a disincentive to reporting workplace injuries and illnesses.

5. Remember, providing trivial rewards for outstanding safety performance is a disincentive for working safely.

Influence: The Motivation Stage

Who	Safety and human resource department.
What	Employees must be rewarded for their safety achievements.
When	After any safety achievement and/or organizational success.
Why	Organizations should always celebrate safety achievement and successes.
How	At this stage an organization should celebrate safety achievements and successes. Most employees want approval and recognition. So reward safe behavior. Monetary rewards may become an inducement to under-reporting, but rewards should make people feel valued and valuable.

Table 13

Chapter 19

Indicate

You can't manage what you can't measure.
—PETER DRUCKER

Key Concepts: Monitor/Measure/Evaluation/Benchmarking/Accountability

Let's face it...safety is difficult! In many organizations, safety is usually measured on negative results such as the number of injuries or incidents. It has been said that *safety* is the measure of failures—the number of injuries or incidents, the lost time accident rate, or the experience modification rate. While true that safety is often measured on statistics and numbers that represent failure, these trailing or lagging indicators have value.

This ingredient of "Indicate" addresses the monitoring, measuring, evaluating, benchmarking, and holding people accountable for safety performance in the organization. Indicate is the one special ingredient in the safety management system recipe that will help prevent injuries in the workplace, because it deals with safety accountability.

Value is a difficult thing to measure in general, and the value of safety is no different. How do you know how many incidents or fatalities you prevented with your safety measures? Organizations need to recognize that there is no single reliable measure of health and safety performance. Using a multitude of measures will provide a better gauge

Indicators to measure the safety system's success. Management needs to be able to measure success and keep score with tangible, measurable metrics. Effective management of the safety management system cannot occur without measurement. At a minimum, management should annually evaluate the health and safety system.

of the effectiveness of the SMS. There is much discussion in the literature about the use of trailing indicators, current indicators, and leading indicators. All are important and have value in monitoring, measuring, and evaluating the organization's SMS.

There is an axiom that states, "What gets measured gets done." Managers are generally concerned about the dollars the organization makes and spends—and rightfully so. That is why they use balance sheets, profit and loss statements, and other such accounting documents to measure success and keep score. Safety and health should be no different. Great managers deliver measurable results. They do it by getting the right things done, motivating staff, and attracting other top performers like themselves to participate in the SMS.

The leaders of an organization must guard against complacency. How do managers gauge whether their safety management system is getting stronger or losing stream? Conducting employee perception surveys, administering regular health and safety inspections, reviewing workers' compensation loss runs, and OSHA 300 logs are just some of the ways an organization can tell if the SMS is getting stronger or getting weaker. Management should also be aware of worker behaviors that compromise safety, such as poor housekeeping.

We have established that effective management of the SMS cannot occur without measurement. Management needs to be able to measure success and keep score with tangible, measurable metrics. Developing safety metrics is the key to protecting your employees and the bottom line. A metric is a standard of measurement. Safety metrics are excellent tools to uncover problems before they negatively impact your employees and your organization's bottom line. When you know what to measure, your organization can prevent expensive mistakes by fixing problems before they happen.

But what should you be measuring? You want to measure safety performance toward some goal. Choose the best safety metrics for your organization and try to tie them into organizational goals. Focus on continuous improvement. You should measure your safety performance in relationship to business goals. Be sure to ask your employees what they think is important. If you are not you measuring the performance of your safety culture, then you are missing out on a huge opportunity. You can spend hours tracking leading and lagging indicators and charting your results and still not see a noticeable decline in incidents, illnesses, and injuries. The best safety metrics are the ones that you customize to your organization. There is no one best approach.

I believe it is extremely beneficial to benchmark your safety efforts against others in your industry. Benchmarking will allow you to evaluate your safety performance in relationship to other organizations. Seek out the best companies to benchmark against and try to match them, but don't try to emulate them. Sources for benchmarking include the Bureau of Labor Statistics (BLS) and the National Safety Council.

As stated previously, when you know what to measure, your organization can prevent expensive mistakes by fixing safety problems before they occur. But the key is to know what to measure. Here are several key safety and health metrics for tracking the performance of safety and health programs:

- Occupational Safety and Health Administration (OSHA) Injury and Illness Incident Report and Summary

- Lost Workday Incidence Rate

- OSHA Days Away from Work, Restricted Work, or Job Transfer Injury and Illness Rate (DART rate)

- Person-hours worked since last lost workday incident

- Number and amount of OSHA fines

- Workers' compensation experience modifier

From a regulatory compliance standpoint, OSHA expects companies to keep OSHA required records of work-related injuries and illnesses. This data is gathered on the OSHA 300 log. Regulatory compliance may keep the OSHA Compliance Safety and Health Officer (CSHO) out of your kitchen, but compliance alone will not reduce or eliminate injuries or illnesses over the long haul. And while we are talking about OSHA 300 logs, it has been my experience that it is advisable to have at least five years' worth of logs readily available if and when a CSHO visits your establishment. Typically during an inspection this is one of the first things the CSHO will ask for, along with supporting accident or incident reports. It is advisable *not* to have the compliance officer wait around impatiently while you fumble looking for records. The tone of the inspection can be set—good or bad—on how efficiently you can produce the logs and supporting documentation.

There is lots of discussion in the literature today about whether to measure your system using leading and lagging or trailing indicators. You need to know how to measure what matters most to drive safety in your organization.

Lagging or trailing indicators, such as incidence rates, measure what has already happened. Leading indicators attempt to capture what is happening now to prevent injuries or incidents in the future. An effective leading indicator is an employee perception survey. A complete and accurate picture of your safety management system emerges by correlating leading indicators with appropriate lagging indicators.

OSHA's Form 300A (Rev. 01/2004)

Summary of Work-Related Injuries and Illnesses

All establishments covered by Part 1904 must complete this Summary page, even if no work-related injuries or illnesses occurred during the year. Remember to review the Log to verify that the entries are complete and accurate before completing this summary.

Using the Log, count the individual entries you made for each category. Then write the totals below, making sure you've added the entries from every page of the Log. If you had no cases, write "0."

Employees, former employees, and their representatives have the right to review the OSHA Form 300 in its entirety. They also have limited access to the OSHA Form 301 or its equivalent. See 29 CFR Part 1904.35, in OSHA's recordkeeping rule, for further details on the access provisions for these forms.

Number of Cases			
Total number of deaths	Total number of cases with days away from work	Total number of cases with job transfer or restriction	Total number of other recordable cases
_____	_____	_____	_____
(G)	(H)	(I)	(J)

Figure 11 OSHA's Form 300A, which summarizes the total number of job-related injuries and illnesses that occurred during the year are logged on OSHA Form 300, Log of Work-Related Injuries and Illnesses.

Be sure you are gathering the right data. Ensure the proper interpretation of your data. Sometimes we may over-analyze that data, and that will lead to poorly aligning safety goals with organizational goals.

You must create a balance in safety performance measurement systems—including a balance between leading and lagging measures and a balance among the types of leading measures (including activity and outcome measures). You must understand both the limitations and the meaningful application of lagging/trailing measures. Use leading measures to motivate, drive performance, and foster continuous improvement in your organization. Leading indicators that can be measured are:

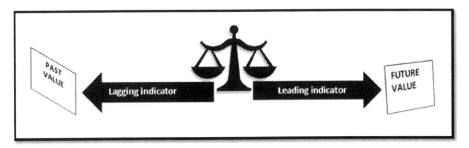

Figure 12

- The frequency of employee safety training
- Safety communications
- Job hazard analysis completed
- Near miss reporting
- Safety inspection reports
- Safety committee objectives achieved
- Audit scores
- Incident investigations completed timely
- Observed safe behaviors
- Employee perception surveys on climate

An organization must routinely check on progress and provide feedback on performance against safety-related roles and goals. Use audit results as one key measure of your organization's safety performance improvement. You must be very careful that your accountability system does not place blame or have harsh negative consequences.

While the goal is to never have a work-related injury or illness, sometimes it does happen. When an employee loses time from work and/or incurs medical bills, in almost all cases, they will receive workers' compensation benefits. Organizations that have created a post-injury management system to outline how they oversee work-related injuries and illness will better manage costs associated with the accident then those that don't. Workers' compensation data is a key safety and health metric.

There is no single indicator that will give you the status of your safety management system. It is a multitude of indictors that best let management measure success and gauge the effectiveness of the system.

You must do something with the data you get from your measurements; otherwise it means nothing. It is what you do with the data and information that matters most. When managers make safety a key indicator and give it the same weight as other company functions such as production, quality, and finance, they will often find that their organizations have achieved excellent performance. If you properly incorporated all twelve ingredients of the iforSafety methodology, you should have a fully integrated sustainable safety system in your organization.

There must be regular management review of the safety management system. At a minimum, senior management must review the safety management system annually. It should be reviewed to ensure its continued suitability and effectiveness in supporting injury prevention, injury management and improved safety outcomes.

How do I know this works? Brigadier General Timothy J. Edens, from the U.S. Army Combat Readiness/Safety Center, said in an article written for the Army's website that, "One of the perennial questions in safety is, "How do we measure what we're doing?" In the article he states:

> Too often, the only metric we have available is how many soldiers died in accidents during any particular period. We've gotten into the habit of looking at those numbers and attributing our safety programs' success or failure to them. This isn't necessarily a bad thing; we obviously want the arrow pointing downward on accidental deaths. But, I don't believe it's enough to quantify what we do every day with only a single figure—safety is much bigger and more complex than that.

> …In my mind, metrics should be about accountability, not simply numbers. Getting your unit to 100 percent on training requirements or mandated inspections is a noble goal, but it never falls to a single person or event to do it. We must hold our leaders to task in meeting stated metrics, not just the safety officer and not merely against the number of fatalities to accidents. The same is true for developing metrics; every leader should be involved in the process, and honestly, soldiers should be too. Talking to your troops will give you a good idea of reasonable goals, and then, based on your experience and judgment, you can dial up the "hard" in the process. Simply making a command decision to reduce accidents by whatever percentage won't make a workable goal or create an environment where your soldiers buy in to safety through their own participation in risk management. Properly developed safety metrics can

be part of your unit's safety culture, provide incentive, and inspire achievement.[65]

In order to properly manage your safety system, you need to continuously measure and oversee the system. Realize that there is no amount of measuring that will improve an SMS. It requires action from the leaders of the organization to see improvement in the system. If measuring safety success works for the U.S. Army, it can work for your organization! So how can you assess the current status of your safety management system? Learn how in the next chapter.

SAFETY IN ACTION:

1. Choose the best safety metrics for your organization.

2. Use a mix of lagging, current and leading indicators.

3. Develop an effective performance measurement system to improve safety and correct problems.

4. Define desired results of safety initiatives and activities.

5. Show the return-on-investment (ROI) of your safety initiatives using key metrics.

6. Keep score. Measure your safety success.

7. Evaluate the system regularly (at least annually) and take necessary corrective action.

---

[65] Brig. Gen. Timothy J. Edens, US Army Combat Readiness/Safety Center. "From the Director of Army Safety—Measuring Up." (February 1, 2013). http://www.army.mil/article/95547/From_the_Director_of_Army_Safety___Measuring_Up/.

Indicate: The Evaluation Stage

Who	Senior management, safety department, supervisors and employees.
What	An organization must measure the effectiveness of its safety management system to know if it is getting stronger or losing steam. Additionally an organization is required to keep OSHA required records of work-related injuries and illnesses.
When	Conduct regular health and safety inspections and audits. Regularly review sections of the safety management system. Annually evaluate the entire safety management system.
Why	At this stage organizations should be conducting perception surveys and benchmarking their safety performance. This helps to guard against complacency.
How	Employee engagement studies and employee perception surveys, OSHA 300 logs, workers compensation data, are just a few of the many ways to measure safety performance.

Table 14

Chapter 20

Assessing Your Safety Management System— Take the iExam for FREE

What is essential is invisible to the eye.
—FROM THE LITTLE PRINCE

The iforSafety methodology is a simple and systemic way of managing an organization's health and safety affairs to improve safety performance and raise the awareness of the value of safety.

DO A FREE SELF-ASSESSMENT OF YOUR SAFETY SYSTEM

The iExam is a Web-based assessment that determines which ingredients of a safety system your organization is missing or could be done better. It is very easy and can be completed in less than forty-five minutes. The questions range from basic to complex, but the substance of these questions is recognized in the industry as being necessary to determine the performance level of the safety system. You will learn what you don't know and what you do know about your company's safety culture. And, from there, you will have a starting point to improve the culture. Our Recommendations for Improvement can be used as a starting point to facilitate discussion and bring positive change in your company. We call this "seeing the light," because this is where the light bulb gets switched on for many organizations.

WHAT CAN TAKING THE IEXAM DO FOR YOU?

One of the most important safety performance improvement steps that you and your leadership team can take is to assess your safety management system by conducting a gap analysis between your present safety system and the iforSafety safety improvement process. The iforSafety model provides an organization detailed instructions and tools necessary for implementing a successful system that will not only comply with OSHA requirements, but will also improve performance and positively impact the bottom line.

The exam will help you assess the maturity of your current safety system, and it is your first step to truly making a difference in the performance of your safety system. It identifies organizational and management attributes that contribute to a strong and sustainable safety culture. The iExam defines the level of proficiency or maturity for each ingredient. Recommendations are made to help you move to the next ingredient. The assessment and scoring is by no means scientific. It is based on personal experience, professional training, and education. However, this assessment can be a useful tool to help you gauge the organization's commitment to safety based on twelve strategic principles. It is well documented that an increased focus on health and safety, and following these principles, translates into a safer, healthier workplace.

What do your *i*'s say about your safety management system? It is important to understand where your organization currently is in the development of a safety management system. The iExam will help clarify where your safety system is currently performing. The iExam can help you determine your current condition and help you start thinking about how you would like your safety system to perform in the future.

IEXAM SCORE RESULTS INDICATE LEVEL OF SAFETY SYSTEM PROFICIENCY (SUCCESS)

When you receive your iExam score, the results indicate the overall effectiveness of the safety system. The assessment then measures your strengths and weaknesses for twelve key ingredients in creating a sustainable safety system. The Recommendations for Improvement is your action plan for targeting each ingredient. Use the iExam to establish a baseline of your company's safety performance. As recommendations are implemented, you can retest to measure your progress over time. As mentioned above, the overall score on the iExam constitutes the level at which your company's health and safety system is scored. This level is an informal assessment of the system based on the responses provided by the person taking the assessment. The score does *not* represent a compliance judgment, meaning it does *not* determine whether your company is in compliance with OSHA regulations.

WHERE DO I GO TO TAKE THE IEXAM?

The data collected will be used to understand how organizations manage their safety management systems. The demographic information required by the individual to take the iExam is strictly confidential and is not shared with any other organizations.

Visit the website *www.health-safetysolutions.com* and follow the instructions to launch the iExam. Fill out the demographic information and start taking the exam that helps you assess the current status of your safety management system. Taking the exam will allow your organization to view your safety culture through a different set of eyes. See what could be!

By following the Recommendations for Improvement—which are current best management practices—and by creating an action plan, this will help close the gap. The action plan can serve as a road map to get your health and safety system to where it should be. It makes good business sense to reduce the cost and risks associated with workplace incidents by ensuring that safety and health becomes an *integral* part of the business. The iExam provides a framework, guiding you through an approach that has proven successful. Put safety in your line of vision to create a healthier, more productive workforce. Don't miss out on this i-catching opportunity.

Epilogue

"Obstacles are the things we see when we take our eyes off our goals."
- ZIG ZIGLAR

Well, there you have it, ladies and gentlemen—a recipe to follow with twelve essential ingredients that will contribute to the creation of a strong and sustainable safety management system. No secret sauces, just practical real-life information. Safety management will be easier, and worries about OSHA inspections less threatening, when you follow this process. Yes, safety can be difficult, but if you have a plan and follow that plan, things will be so much easier. Some say you can never achieve 100 percent safety. I'll let you be the judge. I say 95 percent safe is a whole lot better than 50 percent safe. Strive for perfection! If one safety professional, one person responsible for safety, one human resource manager, one CEO, or one business owner reads this book, creates a safety management system, and it saves just *one* life, then it was well worth the effort of writing this book.

Based on my experience, education, review of the literature, and research, it is generally accepted that safety professionals are responsible to make safety a company priority by effectively pro-moting the function using influence, spreading enthusiasm, and by using other essential skills. However, for safety professionals or the people responsible for safety to successfully "get over the wall" and effectively lead the safety effort, they need the unwavering support of senior management. It has been long recognized that the person responsible for safety efforts alone cannot achieve company-wide safety success. The following twelve recommendations are directed toward senior management:

1. Recognize that workers' compensation expense is *not* just a cost of doing business.
2. Recognize that management has the control (financial resources) to reduce the number of on-the-job injuries and illnesses.
3. Take the attitude that injuries are generally the direct result of a breakdown in the management system.
4. Reward employees for working safely and celebrate safety achievement and successes.
5. Treat employees as assets to the company—*not liabilities.*
6. Do *not* have your management team be a team of "firefighters." Be a proactive organization instead of one that is always reactive. "Sometimes nothing happens until something happens." Don't make this your organization's motto.
7. Take a broader view of safety.
8. Everyone in the organization needs to shoulder the responsibility for the organizational safety culture.
9. Safety should be a *process* not a *program*, or management gets the level of safety it deserves.
10. Be an organization in which safety is on the cutting edge.
11. Conduct incident investigations as fact-finding missions, not fault-finding missions.

12. Escape the "ivory tower" regularly and *see* what *really* is happening.[66]

Build relationships, get management buy-in, engage employees, invest in safety, train, communicate, investigate, inspect, measure, reward performance, and hold people accountable. Managing safety will be less difficult and regulatory compliance will be much simpler, when you use the iforSafety methodology. That's the recipe. It's *not* that difficult. What are you waiting for…you read the recipe…so start cooking! Make safety the "in" thing at your organization!

---

[66] Miozza, Michael L. *Safety in a Changing World* . Fall River, Massachusetts (©2001): 187–195.

Sources of Information and Other Interesting Reading

22 Ways That Will Make You a Champion for Safety! by David Lynn and David J. Sarkus (2006)

Accident Investigation Techniques by Jeffrey S. Oakley (2012)

Building a Better Safety and Health Committee by John P. Spath, CSP (1998)

Creating & Maintaining a Practical Based Safety Culture by Alan D. Quilley CRSP (2012)

Developing Safety Training Programs: Preventing Accidents and Improving Worker Performance through Quality Training by Joseph A. Saccaro (1994)

How to Hold Great Safety Meetings: These meetings don't suck anymore! by Alan D. Quilley CRSP (2011)

Inside Out: Rethinking Traditional Safety Management Systems by Larry Wilson and Gary A. Higbee (2012)

Job Hazard Analysis: A Guide for Voluntary Compliance and Beyond by James E. Roughton and Nathan Crutchfield (2008)

Out of the Box: Skills for Developing Your Own Career Path by Mark D. Hansen, American Society of Safety engineers (2002)

Out of the Box: More Skills for Developing Your Own Career Path by Mark D. Hansen, American Society of Safety Engineers (2010)

Removing Obstacles to Safety: A Behavior-Based Approach by Judy Agnew and Gail Snyder (2008)

Safe By Accident? Take the Luck out of Safety by Judy Agnew and Aubrey Daniels (2010)

Safety 24/7: Building an Incident-Free Culture by Gregory M. Anderson & Robert L. Lorber, Ph.D. (2006)

Safety Incentives: The Pros and Cons of Award and Recognition Programs by Wayne G. Pardy (1999)

Safety Matters! by Adrian Flynn and John Shaw of Phoenix Safety (2008)

Safety Metrics: Tools and Techniques for Measuring Safety Performance by Christopher A. Janicak (2003)

Safety Training that Delivers: How to Design and Present Better Technical Training by Sheila Cullen Cantonwine (1999)

Spice It Up! 52 Easy Ways to Turn Your Safety Meetings from Bland to Grand! by Richard Hawk (2003)

The Emperor Has No Hard Hat: Achieving Real Workplace Safety Results by Alan D. Quilley CRSP (2012)

The Manager's Guide to Workplace Safety by R. Scott Stricoff and Donald R. Groover (2012)

The Power of Habit: Why We Do What We Do In Life and Business by Charles Duhigg (2012)

The Safety Coach®: Unleash the 7C's for World-Class Safety Performance! by David J. Sarkus (2001)

The Safety Incentives Answer Book: The Employer's that Answers Evert Safety Incentives Question by Mark Moran (2002)

The Zero Index: A Path to Sustainable Safety Excellence by Behavioral Science Technology, Inc. (2012)

To Be Safe, You Should Assess Your Safety Culture by Thomas E. Williams CPRO, CSS (2012)

Why Employees Don't Do What They're Supposed to and What to do About It by Ferdinard F. Fournies (2007)

Would You Watch Out for My Safety? Helping Others Avoid Personal Injury by John W. Drebinger Jr. (2011)

Appendix B

Sample JSA

<table>
<tr><td colspan="2">JOB SAFETY ANALYSIS</td><td colspan="2">JSABuilder</td></tr>
<tr><td colspan="2">JSA No. JSABuilder Sample Library - 4 (short)</td><td colspan="2"></td></tr>
<tr><td colspan="2">Job/Operation Title:
Electric Arc Welding</td><td colspan="2">Date:</td></tr>
<tr><td colspan="2">Department/Division/Section:
Facility Maintenance</td><td colspan="2">Analysis Developed By:
Name Person 2</td></tr>
<tr><td colspan="2">Location(s):
Welding Shop</td><td colspan="2">Analysis Reviewed By:
Name Person 3</td></tr>
<tr><td colspan="2">Person(s) Performing This Job:
Name Person 1
Name Person 2</td><td colspan="2">Supervisor:
Name Person 1</td></tr>
<tr><td colspan="2">Job Start Date:</td><td colspan="2">Duration:
2 hours</td></tr>
<tr><td>Task/Step</td><td>Potential Hazards</td><td colspan="2">Recommended Safe Job Procedures</td></tr>
<tr><td>1. Sign in and inspect (Step 1)</td><td>- Welding/Cutting/Burning Equipment
- Wires, cables, hoses</td><td colspan="2">- Before setting up the welding shop, visit the Admin desk to sign in.
- Inspect arc welding equipment cables and connections; look for loose connections, frayed insulation on electrode holders and cables (see photo), make sure electrical cables are dry (complete safety checklist).</td></tr>
<tr><td colspan="4">Step 1 Image:
</td></tr>
<tr><td>2. Steps 2 - 6</td><td>- x-- NA ---x</td><td colspan="2">Steps 2 - 6 have been removed to keep this sample to a reasonable length.</td></tr>
<tr><td>3. Perform the weld (Step 7)</td><td>- Arc rays
- Combustible materials
- Electrical equipment (transformers, switching gear, breakers, high voltage lines)
- Ignitable materials and liquids
- Infrared (IR)
- Light (optical) radiation (i.e.</td><td colspan="2">- User proper PPE (see photo).
- Follow manufacturer recommended procedures, lessons learned and experience.
- If possible, position shelf so that head is not in fumes while welding.
- If possible use sub arc process to minmimize light and fumes, and/or minimize the production of welding fumes by using the lowest acceptable amperage and holding the</td></tr>
</table>

	welding operations, etc.). - Repetitive motion or other ergonomic concerns - Rolling or pinching objects - Sharp objects - Slag splatter - Sparks - Ultraviolet (UV) - WELDING FUMES AND GASES - Welding/Cutting/Burning Equipment - Wires, cables, hoses	electrode perpendicular and as close to the work surface and possible. - Keep electrode moving. Tack as appropriate for project and metal type. - Finish the weld.
Step 3 image: 		
4. Steps 8 - 9	- x--- NA ---x	Steps 8 - 9 have been removed to keep this sample to a reasonable length.
5. Remove excess slag from welded material (Step 10)	- Electrical equipment (transformers, switching gear, breakers, high voltage lines) - Hand tools - metal chips - Repetitive motion or other ergonomic concerns - Sharp objects - Sparks - Wires, cables, hoses	When welded material has cooled, use chipping hammer or grinder to remove excess slag from weld (see photo). Secure material to workbench with clamps as necessary, before chipping. FACE SHIELD IS REQUIRED FOR THIS ACTIVITY TO PROTECT FROM FLYING DEBRIS. Be alert to fingers and pinch points and struck-by potential.
Step 5 image:		

6. Steps 11 - 12	- x--- NA ---x	Steps 11 - 12 have been removed to keep this sample to a reasonable length.

POTENTIAL HAZARDS OF THIS JOB

Physical Hazards	Consequences
Combustible materials Electrical equipment (transformers, switching gear, breakers, high voltage lines) Hand tools hot electrodes Ignitable materials and liquids Inadequate lighting Light (optical) radiation (i.e. welding operations, etc.). metal chips Poor Housekeeping Repetitive motion or other ergonomic concerns Rolling or pinching objects Sharp objects Slag splatter Sparks Welding/Cutting/Burning Equipment Wires, cables, hoses x--- NA ---x	Awkward or static position Cuts and abrasions Electrocution or shock Excessive lifting, twisting, pushing, pulling, reaching, or bending Exposure (inhaling, swallowing, or absorbing) to harmful levels of gases, vapors, aerosols, liquids, fumes, or dust) Exposure to excessive light (welding) Falling (< 6 feet), tripping, or slipping Injury caused by slip, trip or fall Pinches Slag splatter Sparks Struck by falling or flying object Struck by uncontrolled pressure release Thermal burns

Chemical Hazards	Description/Health Hazards
WELDING FUMES AND GASES ()	Welding smoke is a mixture of very fine particles (fumes) and gases. Many of the substances in welding smoke, such as chromium, nickel, arsenic, asbestos, manganese, silica, beryllium, cadmium, nitrogen oxides,phosgene, acrolein, fluorine compounds, carbon monoxide, cobalt, copper, lead, ozone, selenium, and zinc can be extremely toxic. Generally, welding fumes and gases come from: - base material being welded or the filler material that is used;

	- coatings and paints on the metal being welded, or coatings covering the electrode; - shielding gases supplied from cylinders; The health effects of welding exposures are difficult to list, because the fumes may contain so many different substances that are known to be harmful (depending on the factors listed above). The individual components of welding smoke can affect just about any part of the body, including the lungs, heart, kidneys, and central nervous system. (Welding Hazard Safety Program, TX Dept of Insurance)
Radiological Hazards	**Description/Health Hazards**
Arc rays Infrared (IR) Ultraviolet (UV) Visible light	Effect on the Eyes - Welder's flash (feeling of sand or grit in eyes, blurred vision, intense pain, burning, and headache) Effects on the Eyes - Cataracts Effects on the Skin - Burns momentary blinding

HAZARD CONTROL MEASURES USED FOR THIS JOB	
Administrative Controls: Certified operators Competent person Drug and alcohol policy Emergency procedures Equipment maintenance and servicing manual Ergonomic procedure Hot work procedure Housekeeping practices Inspections (ongoing) work areas, equipment, tools, etc. Inspections (pre-job) - work areas, equipment, tools, etc. Material Safety Data Sheets (MSDS) Monitoring (hazardous atmospheres) Operating instructions (equipment) Operating procedures (process) Radiological safety program Safety checklists (use to document inspections)	*Required Training:* Ergonomics Fire protection (extinguishers) General Safety Hazard Communication (HAZCOM) Orientation (site or job) Personal protective equipment (PPE) Respiratory protection Welding, cutting, and brazing
Engineering Controls: Ventilation and exhausting.	*Required PPE:* Boots - compatible for OSHA electrical protection requirements Clothing - fire resistant Clothing - long pants Clothing - long sleeve shirt Fire resistant gauntlet glove Safety glasses: see manual for lens shade requirements for welder & spotter Side shield Welding hood Welding jacket & apron
Required Permit(s): No permit required - verify no LOTO is in progress on chosen equipment Welding shop - space reservation (see Admin desk for list of welding operations & times)	*Other Information:* A 2A20B:C fire extinguisher must be readily available and within arm's reach at all times. Fire alarm operability must be confirmed prior to start of work. Follow manufacturer instructions to test fire alarm. Also, follow all manufacturer instructions for operation of the electic arc welder. STOP WORK immediately if an unsafe or potentially unsafe condition exists.

This sample created at www.JSABuilder.com.

Appendix C
Sample Safety Committee Guidelines

1.0 INTRODUCTION

XXXX is committed to accident prevention in order to protect the safety and health of all our employees. Injury and illness losses due to hazards are needless, costly, and preventable. To prevent these losses, a joint management/worker safety committee will be established. Employee involvement in accident prevention and support of safety committees' members and activities is necessary to ensure a safe and healthful workplace.

2.0 PURPOSE

The purpose of our safety committee is to bring workers and management together in a cooperative effort to promote safety and health in the workplace. The safety committee will assist management and make recommendations for change.

3.0 ORGANIZATION

There shall be both employee and management representatives serving on the safety committee. Employee representatives shall be volunteers or elected by their peers. If no employee volunteers are elected, management may appoint them. Management representatives will be appointed. Safety committee members will serve a continuous term of at least one-year.

Length of membership will be staggered so that at least one experienced member is always serving on the committee. Committee members must make a commitment to attend all meetings. At times, business reasons may preclude someone from attending or showing up on time. Any committee member missing two (2) meetings or late more than ten (10) minutes (which would constitute a miss) in a year will be removed from the committee.

In order to minimize distractions, meeting attendees should respectfully place cell phones and pagers on silent mode.

4.0 EXTENT OF AUTHORITIES

The safety committee advises management on issues that will promote safety and health in the workplace. Written recommendations are expected from the safety committee, and they will be submitted to management. In turn, management will give serious consideration to the recommendations submitted, and will respond in writing to the committee in a reasonable time frame.

5.0 FUNCTIONS

1. *Management Commitment to Workplace Safety and Health*

   A. Establish procedures for review and management's response to minutes.

B. Respond in writing to committee recommendations.

C. Submit written recommendations for safety and health improvements.

D. Review corrective action taken by management.

E. Evaluate XXXX safety and health policies and procedures.

2. *Committee Meetings and Employee Involvement*

A. Establish procedures for employee input, i.e. to receive suggestions, report hazards, and other pertinent safety and health information.

B. Develop and make available written agenda for each meeting.

C. Take meeting minutes and distribute to committee members and management.

D. Include employee input on agenda for safety committee meeting.

E. Include in the meeting minutes all recommendations for improvement.

F. Keep meeting minutes for three (3) years.

G. Hold monthly meetings (except months when quarterly inspections are done).

3. *Hazard Assessment and Control*

A. Establish procedures for workplace inspections to identify safety and health hazards. The following is *not* a complete list, but is a range of possible hazards:

HEALTH	SAFETY
Fumes and vapors	Unguarded machinery
Dust	Machinery in need of maintenance
Excessive heat or cold	Inadequate or unmarked emergency exits
Noise and vibration	Poor lighting
Spilled chemicals	Electrical hazards
Radiation	Mishandling of chemicals or flammable substances
Physical stress	Poor housekeeping

B. Appoint an inspection team of at least one (1) plant/office representative and one (1) management representative.

C. Conduct workplace safety inspections at least quarterly.

D. Make written report of hazard location discovered during quarterly inspection.

E. Review corrective measures for adequacy. Make written recommendations to correct hazards and submit to management for timely response.

4. Safety and Health Planning

A. Review procedures and inspection reports and make appropriate implementation of any new safety and health rules and work practices.

B. Assist XXXX in evaluating the accident and illness prevention program.

C. Develop and establish procedures to conduct annual review of XXXX's accident prevention program.

D. Anticipate unforeseen problems when changes in operations occur or a new facility is built. Make recommendations to prevent any safety or health problems that may result.

5. Accountability

A. Evaluate XXXX's safety and health accountability systems.

B. Make recommendations to implement supervisor/manager and worker accountability for safety and health.

6. Accident and Incident Investigations

A. Establish procedures for investigating all safety incidents, including injury accidents, illness, and death, so that recommendations can be made for appropriate corrective action to prevent recurrence.

B. Review accident investigation reports to determine problem areas requiring immediate attention and appoint management personnel for correcting.

C. Follow-up on corrective action(s) taken on recommendations of previous meeting.

7. Safety and Health Training

A. Provide training for workers and supervisors/managers to ensure knowledge of safe lifting techniques, etc.

B. Ergonomic training for supervisors/managers to assist them in setting up safe workstations for their employees.

6.0 RECOMMENDATIONS

All recommendations submitted to management must be written and should:

- Be clear and concise
- Provide reasons for implementation
- Show implementation and recommended completion dates
- List benefits to be gained

7.0 PROCEDURES

The committee's plan of action requires procedures by which the committee may successfully fulfill its role. Procedures developed should include but are not limited to:

- Meeting date, time, and location
- Election of chairperson and secretary
- Order of business
- Records
- Duties of each member must include, but are not limited to:
    - Reporting unsafe conditions and practices
    - Attending all safety committee meetings
    - Review all accidents and near misses
    - Recommending ideas for improving safety and health
    - Being a role model by working safely and healthfully
    - Observing how safety and health is enforced in the workplace
    - Completing assignments given by the chairperson
    - Acting as a work area representative in matters pertaining to safety and health
    - Others as determined by XXXX's safety and health needs

8.0 SUMMARY

Only the planning and effective joint leadership of management and the safety committee can build a safety system that will last and is effective. The safety committee shall be a constructive entity, providing guidance and leadership in matters pertaining to the overall health and safety of the facility it represents. Only with this kind of commitment to teamwork can we attain the goal of making XXXX the safest company in the world.

APPENDIX D

Hierarchy of Safety and Health Controls

Most Effective	1) Elimination or Substitution	• substitute fro hazardous material • reduce speed, force, amperage • reduce pressure, temperature • change process to eliminate noise • perform task at ground level • automated material handling
	2) Engineering Controls	• ventilation systems • machine guarding • sound enclosures • circuit breakers • platforms and guard railing • interlocks • lift tables, conveyors, balancers
	3) Warnings	• computer warning • odor in natural gas • signs • backup alarms • beepers • horns • labels
	4) Training and Procedures Administrative Controls	• safe job procedures • rotation of workers • safety equipment inspections • Hazard Communication Training • Lockout • Confined Space Entry
Least Effective	5) Personal Protective Equipment	• safety glasses • ear plugs • face shields • safety harness and lanyards • Back belts

Adopted from various sources to include the Center for Diseases Control and Prevention - Engineering Controls - NIOSH Workplace Safety and Health Topic". Cdc.gov. Retrieved 2012-04-11.

APPENDIX E

OSHA Poster

Job Safety and Health

It's the law!

OSHA®
Occupational Safety
and Health Administration
U.S. Department of Labor

EMPLOYEES:

- You have the right to notify your employer or OSHA about workplace hazards. You may ask OSHA to keep your name confidential.

- You have the right to request an OSHA inspection if you believe that there are unsafe and unhealthful conditions in your workplace. You or your representative may participate in that inspection.

- You can file a complaint with OSHA within 30 days of retaliation or discrimination by your employer for making safety and health complaints or for exercising your rights under the OSH Act.

- You have the right to see OSHA citations issued to your employer. Your employer must post the citations at or near the place of the alleged violations.

- Your employer must correct workplace hazards by the date indicated on the citation and must certify that these hazards have been reduced or eliminated.

- You have the right to copies of your medical records and records of your exposures to toxic and harmful substances or conditions.

- Your employer must post this notice in your workplace.

- You must comply with all occupational safety and health standards issued under the OSH Act that apply to your own actions and conduct on the job.

EMPLOYERS:

- You must furnish your employees a place of employment free from recognized hazards.

- You must comply with the occupational safety and health standards issued under the OSH Act.

This free poster available from OSHA –
The Best Resource for Safety and Health

Free assistance in identifying and correcting hazards or complying with standards is available to employers, without citation or penalty, through OSHA-supported consultation programs in each state.

1-800-321-OSHA (6742)
www.osha.gov

OSHA 3165-02 2012R

APPENDIX F

Do This...Not That!

INGREDIENT	DO THIS!	NOT THAT!
INVENT	Be visible—walk the talk!	Sit in the ivory tower.
INVEST	Provide the necessary resources.	Skimp on safety.
INTRODUCE	Make safety expectations clear on the first day.	Be overwhelming with information.
INTEGRATE	Make safety a core company value.	Treat safety as an added activity.
INFORM	Provide meaningful communication on a regular basis.	Make communication a one-way street.

INSTRUCT	Provide safety training based on the employees' exposure to certain hazards.	Allow untrained employees to operate machinery, equipment, or tools.
INVOLVE	Remove silos—engage employees.	Allow employees to be directly involved in the safety system.
INSPECT	Create a schedule for regular safety inspections.	Sanitize the inspection results.
INVESTIGATE	Investigate all workplace incidents, including near misses and drill down to understand why the incident occurred.	Place blame for incident.
INTERVENE	Create accountability for the results of the safety management system.	Fail to discipline for a clear infraction of safety procedures.
INFLUENCE	If people are your most valuable asset, then treat them as such.	Neglect to recognize them for their safety achievements.
INDICATE	Measure so you can manage.	Become complacent and *not* regularly review your safety management system.

Appendix G

Sample Written Company Policy Statement

The following statement is not intended to be all-inclusive, nor is it intended to fit the requirements of every employer.

(Facility Name)

Safety Policy Statement

It is the policy of (facility name) to protect the safety and health of our employees. It is in the best interest of our employees in this company to avoid injuries and illnesses. Our facility has established a safety and health program adapted to fundamental occupational safety and health concepts that will help us prevent injury and illness due to hazards. Employee involvement at all levels of the facility is critical for us to be successful in this effort. To accomplish this task, a joint worker/ management safety committee will be established. Its purpose will be to bring workers and management together in a non-adversarial, co-operative effort to promote safety and health in our workplace. Our safety committee will be responsible for making recommendations for change to benefit the health and safety of all our employees.

MANAGEMENT:

Management's responsibility is the prevention of workplace injuries and illnesses. Management provides direction and full support to the super-visors and employees regarding all safety and health procedures, job training, and hazard elimination practices. We must be fully aware of all safety and health issues throughout the facility and review the effec-tiveness of our safety and health program as a routine practice.

SUPERVISION:

Supervisors are directly responsible for job training to ensure that all proper procedures, safe work practices, and methods to do the job are communicated effectively. Supervisors will be held accountable for enforcement of our facility rules and take immediate corrective action to eliminate hazardous conditions and practices.

SAFETY COMMITTEE:

The safety committee consists of management and employee rep-resentatives who have an interest in the general promotion safety and health for (facility name). The committee is responsible for mak-ing recommendations on how to improve safety and health in the workplace. Members of the committee have been charged with re-sponsibility to define problems and remove obstacles to accident prevention, identify hazards and recommend corrective actions, help identify employee safety training needs, and establish accident investigation procedures for our facility.

EMPLOYEES:

Each employee is expected to cooperate and take personal responsibility for his/her own safety and health as well as the safety and health of coworkers. If everyone takes responsibility and does what is necessary to ensure workplace safety and health, we all benefit.

- Accidents must be reported immediately to your supervisor.

- All employees must wear required personal protective equipment.

- Hazardous conditions or other safety and health concerns must be reported to your supervisor immediately.

- Employees should participate in safety committee activities, and support safety committee membership. No job is so important that we cannot take time to do it safely.

Sincerely,

Signature of Owner or CEO

Date

Adopted from Rhode Island Department of Labor and Training, Division of Workers' Compensation, Education Unit, Cranston, Rhode Island (May, 2005 ed.)

Appendix H

Organizations and Agencies

When you are involved in safety, there are a number of organizations and agencies that you will need to know about. Some use major acronyms, like OSHA. These non-word acronyms listed below in parentheses are immensely helpful when communicating about the organizations that keep us safe and healthy.

American Association of Occupational Health Nurses (AAOHN) *www.aaohn.org* | **800-241-8014**

American Board of Industrial Hygiene (ABIH) *www.abih.org* | **517-321-2638**

American Conference of Governmental Industrial Hygienist (ACGHI) *www.acgih.org* | **513-742-6163**

American National Safety Institute (ANSI) *www.ansi.org* | **202-293-8020**

American National Standards Institute (ANSI) *www.ansi.org* | **202-293-8020**

American Red Cross *www.redcross.org* | **800-733-2767**

American Society for Testing and Materials (ASTM) *www.astm.org* | **877-909-2786**

American Society of Mechanical Engineers (ASME) *www.asme.org* | **800-843-2763**

American Society of Safety Engineers (ASSE) *www.asse.org* | **847-699-2929**

Board of Certified Safety Professionals (BCSP) *www.bcsp.org* | **217-359-9263**

Bureau of Labor Statistics (BLS) *www.bls.gov* | **202-691-5200**

Canada Safety Council *www.canadasafetycouncil.org/home* | **613-739-1535**

Canadian Centre for Occupational Health and Safety (CCOSH) *http://www.ccosh.ca* | **800-668-4284**

Canadian Center for Occupational Health and Safety (CCOHS) *www.ccohs.ca* | **905-572-2981**

Canadian Registration Board of Occupational Hygienists (CRBOH) *www.crboh.ca/page.cfm?onumber=1* | **604-276-3302**

Canadian Society of Safety Engineering (CSSC) *www.csse.org* | **416-646-1600**

Centers for Disease Control and Prevention (CDC) *www.cdc.gov* | **800-232-4636**

Citizens Corps *www.citizencorps.gov* | **800-621-3362**

Construction Safety Council *www.buildsafe.org* | **708-544-2082**

Consumer Product Safety Commission (CPSC) *www.cpsc.gov* | **800-638-2772**

Department of Energy (DOE) *www.energy.gov* | **202-586-5000**

Department of Homeland Security *www.ready.gov* | **800-621-3362**

Department of Transportation (DOT) *www.dot.gov* | **866-377-8642**

Environmental Protection Agency (EPA) *www.epa.gov* | **202-564-1643**

Federal Emergency Management Agency (FEMA) *www.fema.gov* | **800-621-3362**

Food and Drug Administration (FDA) *www.fda.gov* | **888-463-6332**

Health and Physics Society *www.hps.org/* | **703-790-1745**

Human Factors and Ergonomics Society (HFES) *www.hfes.org/web/Default.aspx* | **310-394-1811**

Institute for Business and Home Safety (IBHS) *www.disastersafety. org* | **813-286-3400**

Institute of Hazardous Materials Management *www.ihmm.org* | **301-984-8969**

International Standards Organization (ISO) *www.iso.org/iso/home. html* | **+41 22 749 01 11**

Mortality and Morbidity Weekly Reports (MMWR) *www.cdc.gov/ mmwr/* | **800-232-4636**

National Electrical Manufacturers Association (NEMA) *www.nema. org* | **800-341-5266**

National Fire Protection Agency (NFPA) *www.nfpa.org* | **877-918-7957**

National Highway and Traffic Safety Administration (NHTSA) *www. nhtsa.gov* | **888-327-4236**

National Institute for Occupational Safety and Health (NIOSH) *www.cdc.gov/niosh* | **800-232-4636**

National Institutes of Health (NIH) *www.nih.gov/* | **301-496-4000**

National Safety Council (NSC) *www.nsc.org* | **800-621-7615**

National Transportation Board (NTSB) *www.ntsb.gov* | **202-314-6000**

National Weather Service *www.nws.noaa.gov* | **301-713-0622**

Nuclear Regulatory Commission (NRC) *www.nrc.gov* | **800-368-5642**

Occupational and Health Administration (OSHA) *www.osha.gov* | **800-321-6742**

Rocky Mountain Center for Occupational and Environmental Health (RMCOEH) *www.medicine.utah.edu/rmcoeh* | **801-581-4800**

The Institutes *www.theinstitutes.org* | **800- 644-2101**

Underwriters' Laboratories (UL) *www.ul.com* | **877-854-3577**

U.S. Fire Administration (USFA) *www.usfa.dhs.gov* | **301-447-1000**

Appendix I

OSHA Training Requirements

Type of Activity/ Training	29 CFR 1910. General Industry	29 CFR 1926. Construction	Who Receives Training	Frequency of Training
Accident Prevention Signs and Tags	145	200	All employees	Initial / Periodic
Asbestos Abatement Training	1001	1101	Employees exposed to asbestos	Initial / Annual
Asbestos Awareness Training	1001	1101	Employees potentially exposed to asbestos	Initial / Annual
Asbestos Operations and Maintenance Training	1001	1101	Employees exposed to asbestos	Initial / Annual

Type of Activity/ Training	29 CFR 1910. General Industry	29 CFR 1926. Construction	Who Receives Training	Frequency of Training
Bloodborne Pathogens	1030		Employees with occupational exposure, first aid responders, police	Initial / Annual
Chainsaw Safety	266		Employees using chainsaws as part of their job	Initial
Compressed Gas Safety	101		Employees using compressed gases	Initial
Control of Hazardous Energy (Lockout/ Tagout)	147	407, 432	Employees that may service or maintain equipment	Initial / Periodic
Crane, derrick, and hoist safety	Subpart N	550	Employees using/ operating applicable equipment	Initial/ Regularly thereafter
Diving Safety	410		Employees involved in underwater diving	Initial / Periodic
Electrical Safety-Related Work	332	Subpart K	Employees working with electrical equipment	Initial / Periodic

Type of Activity/ Training	29 CFR 1910. General Industry	29 CFR 1926. Construction	Who Receives Training	Frequency of Training
Emergency Action Plan	38	35	All	Initial / Periodic Change in Plan
Explosive or Blasting Agents	109	900	Employees that use, handle, store, or transport, these products	Initial / Periodic
Fall Protection	66 App C	501-503	All exposed workers	Initial / Periodic New Hazard or Equipment
Fire Extinguishing System(s)	160	150	Employees who inspect and/or maintain these systems	Initial / Annual
Fire Prevention Plan	38		All	Initial / Periodic
Formaldehyde	1048(n)		Employees with exposure at or above 0.1 ppm	Initial / Annual

Type of Activity/ Training	29 CFR 1910. General Industry	29 CFR 1926. Construction	Who Receives Training	Frequency of Training
Hazard Communication	1200		All employees exposed to hazardous chemicals (excluding labs), infectious agents, or pesticides	Initial / Periodic New Hazard
Hazardous Waste Management			All employees working with chemicals and generating hazardous waste	Initial
Hazardous Waste Operations and Emergency Response	120	65	Personnel expected to respond to an uncontrolled release	Initial/ Annual
Hearing Protection	95	52	Employees working in high noise areas	Initial / Annual
Job Hazard Analysis	Subpart I, App B		Employees exposed to workplace hazard	Initial/New Hazards
Laboratory Safety	1450		All laboratory employees, new exposures	Initial / refresher every 2 years

Type of Activity/ Training	29 CFR 1910. General Industry	29 CFR 1926. Construction	Who Receives Training	Frequency of Training
Ladder Safety	25, 26, 27	1053	Employees using applicable ladders	Initial/ Change in equipment
Laser Safety			All employees that use lasers (Class 2 or higher)	Initial
Lead	1025	Subpart M	Employees exposed to lead	Initial Assignment / Annual at or above Action Level
Mechanical Power Presses	217		Employees exposed to power presses	Initial / Periodic
Medical Services and First Aid	151	Subpart D	First aid providers and any other employee	Every 2 years for providers; 1 year for others
Methylene Chloride	1052		Employees with exposure	Initial / Annual
New Employee Orientation			All	Initial
Ergonomics (recommended)			Any	Initial
Operations of Powered Platforms	66		Employees using powered platforms	Initial / Periodic

Type of Activity/ Training	29 CFR 1910. General Industry	29 CFR 1926. Construction	Who Receives Training	Frequency of Training
Permit Required Confined Space	146	26(6)	1. Authorized entrants/ attendants, 2. rescue personnel	1. Initial / Periodic 2. Initial/ Annual
Personal Protective Equipment	132	Subpart E	Employees required to use PPE	Initial / Change in work place/ PPE use
Portable Fire Extinguishers	157		Employees with extinguishers in their work area	Initial / Annual
Powered Industrial Trucks	178	602 D	All designated operators or forklifts	Initial / Every 3 years
Process Safety Management of Highly Hazardous Chemicals	119	64	Employees with processes involving a flammable liquid or gas in excess of 10,000 lbs. or a chemical at or above the threshold amount (App A)	
Radiation Safety	NRC requirement		Employees using radioactive materials	Initial

Type of Activity/ Training	29 CFR 1910. General Industry	29 CFR 1926. Construction	Who Receives Training	Frequency of Training
Recordkeeping			(Included in New Employee Orientation)	
Respiratory Protection	134	103	All employees required to wear a respirator of any type	Initial / Annually New Hazard
Scaffold User Safety		451	All employees required to build or work on scaffolds	Initial
Servicing of Multi-Piece and Single-Piece Rim Wheels	177		Maintenance garage employees	Initial / Periodic
Storage and Handling of LP Gases	110	153	All personnel who perform installation, removal, operation or maintenance	Initial / Periodic
Storage of Flammable and Combustible Liquids	106	152	Employees who handle, store, or dispense these products	Initial / Periodic

Type of Activity/ Training	29 CFR 1910. General Industry	29 CFR 1926. Construction	Who Receives Training	Frequency of Training
Toxic and Hazardous Substances	1000		Employees that are exposed at or above the limits for air contaminant listed in Table Z-1*.	Initial / Periodic
Trenching		Subpart P	Employees who work in excavations	Initial / Periodic
Violence in the Workplace (recommended)	General Duty Clause		Any	Initial
Welding	253	Subpart J	All employees who perform welding / cutting operations	Initial / Periodic

The term <u>periodic training</u> generally means training that occurs at regular intervals (e.g. 1 to 3 years).

Appendix J
OSHA Assistance

OSHA can provide extensive help through a variety of programs, including technical assistance about effective safety and health programs, state plans, workplace consultations, voluntary protection programs, strategic partnerships, training and education, and more. An overall commitment to workplace safety and health can add value to your business, your workplace, and your life.

SAFETY AND HEALTH PROGRAM MANAGEMENT GUIDELINES

Effective management of employee safety and health protection is a decisive factor in reducing the extent and severity of work-related injuries and illnesses and their related cost. In fact, an effective safety and health program forms the basis of good employee protection, can save time and money, increase productivity, and reduce employee injuries, illnesses, and related workers' compensation costs.

To assist employers and employees in developing effective safety and health programs, OSHA published recommended Safety and

Health Program Management Guidelines (54 Federal Register (16): 3904—3916, January 26, 1989). These voluntary guidelines apply to all places of employment covered by OSHA.

The guidelines identify four (4) general elements crucial to the development of a successful safety and health management system:

- Management leadership and employee involvement
- Workplace analysis
- Hazard prevention and control
- Safety and health training

The guidelines recommend specific actions, under each of these general elements, to achieve an effective safety and health program. The Federal Register notice is available online at www.osha.gov.

Sample Safety Inspection Checklist

Yes = Satisfactory

No = Needs Improvement

N/A = Not Applicable

(This checklist is intended as a guide to assist managers in conducting a health and safety inspections of the facility. It includes questions relating to general office safety, walking and working surfaces, fire prevention, warehouse, and electrical safety. Questions that receive a No require corrective action.)

Name:			
Facility:		Department:	
Date:			
Signature:			

Deficiency Description	Yes	No	N/A	Location(s) and Corrective Action	Date Corrected
Fire Safety & Prevention					
Are fire extinguishers fully charged and inspected monthly? *(tag, date, initial)*					
Are fire extinguishers unobstructed?					
Are fire alarm pull stations unobstructed?					
Are all electrical panels closed?					
Are extension cords used only in an emergency and for temporary use only?					
Are electrical cords in good condition *(not frayed or taped)*?					
Are doors that are *not* exits, but may be mistaken for exits, marked *"Not an Exit"*?					
Are stairways free of obstructions?					
Are combustible materials *(cardboard boxes, paper)* removed from corridors?					

Deficiency Description	Yes	No	N/A	Location(s) and Corrective Action	Date Corrected
Is an 18" vertical clearance maintained below all sprinkler heads?					
Exits					
Are exit doors unobstructed?					
Are illuminated Exit signs lit properly?					
First Aid					
Are first aid kits accessible and fully stocked?					
Are blood-borne pathogens kits available?					
Is the automated external defibrillator (AED) available and charged?					
Walking & Working Surfaces					
Are carpet/floor tiles secured?					
Is carpeting free of tears, lumps, or trip hazards?					
Are floors free of water or slippery substances?					
Are ceiling tiles secured?					

Deficiency Description	Yes	No	N/A	Location(s) and Corrective Action	Date Corrected
Electrical cords are *not* stretched across aisles or under carpets.					
Emergency & Safety Information					
Is the OSHA poster on display?					
Are evacuation routes posted?					
Are emergency phone numbers posted?					
Is a list of first aid responders posted?					
Is five years of OSHA 300 logs maintained?					
Is the OSHA 300A log posted *(Feb 1 thru Apr 30)*?					
General Work Environment					
Are all work areas clean, sanitary, and orderly?					
Is lighting adequate?					
Are air vents unobstructed?					
Bookcases, Shelves, Cabinets					
Are bookcases & shelves prevented from being overloaded?					

Deficiency Description	Yes	No	N/A	Location(s) and Corrective Action	Date Corrected
Are file drawers closed when *not* in use?					
Chemical Storage and Safety					
Are Material Safety Data Sheets(MSDSs) readily available?					
Is an inventory of chemicals available?					
Emergency Lighting					
Is emergency lightning functioning?					
Warehouse					
Are overhead doors on track?					
Are overhead door panels in good condition *(free of damaged panels)*?					
Is the racking system in good condition *(free of bent or broken legs, uprights, or crossbeams)*?					
Is the roof free of apparent leaks?					
Is access to sprinkler controls unobstructed?					
Are outside premises free from spillage, trash, etc.?					

Deficiency Description	Yes	No	N/A	Location(s) and Corrective Action	Date Corrected
Is the ticket shredder safe to use and all dangerous parts grounded?					
Is the emergency stop on conveyors functioning properly?					
Is the compactor/ baler in good condition?					
Is the warehouse neat and orderly?					
Are empty pallets stored properly *(not on edges or ends)*?					
Does the generator look like it is in good condition?					
Are forklift chargers in good condition *(free from damage)*?					
Does the product look like it is safely stored in the racks?					
Is the emergency eyewash/shower activated and flushed?					
Does the dock-leveler appear to be in good condition?					

Comments & Additional Findings:

Hazards should be corrected as soon as they are identified. For any hazard that cannot be immediately corrected, set a target date for correction based on the probability and severity of an injury or illness resulting from the hazard. Provide interim protection to employees who need it while the correction of the hazard is proceeding.

Appendix L

Safety Days

The following are some of the significant safety observances that occur throughout the calendar year.

March is Workplace Eye Wellness Month and is sponsored by Prevent Blindness America (http://preventblindness.org/)

April 28 is Workers' Memorial Day and is sponsored by the American Federation of Labor & Congress of Industrial Organizations (http://www.alfcio.org)

May 8 is Occupational Safety and Health Professionals Day and is sponsored by the American Society of Safety Engineers (http://www.asse.org/newsroom/naosh)

June is National Safety Month and is sponsored by the National Safety Council (http://nsc.org/nsm)

September is National Preparedness Month and is sponsored by the U.S. Department of Homeland Security (http://www.ready.gov)

There are many more safety observances that occur throughout the year. To obtain a calendar of all the safety events during the year, go to the National Safety Council website and download the Safety Observances Calendar at: http://www.nsc.org/news_resources/Resources/Pages/NSCSafetyCalendar.aspx

Appendix M

Safety Sayings

The following are some "safety sayings" that have had profound meaning to me and that I used regularly throughout my career:

Asking me to overlook a single safety violation would be asking me to compromise the value I have placed on your life!

Safety should never take a holiday, because danger never takes a vacation!

Nobody has the right to deliver the night,

It is time you were stood in front of my face,

Looking into the eyes of my deathly embrace,

And when we meet again, I shall gaze into your soul and ask the question…Why?

"There are only two ways to establish competitive advantages: do things better than others or do them differently."
– KARL ALBRECHT

Thank you. Now go out and establish, repair or fine tune your safety management system.

Made in the USA
Lexington, KY
17 April 2014